Guided MATH Workshop

Authors

Laney Sammons, M.L.S.

Donna Boucher

Foreword

Kimberly Rimbey

SHELL EDUCATION

Publishing Credits

Corinne Burton, M.A.Ed., *Publisher*; Conni Medina, M.A.Ed., *Managing Editor*; Diana Kenney M.A.Ed., *Content Director*; Paula Makridis, *Editor*; Fabiola Sepulveda, *Graphic Designer*; Kyleena Harper, *Assistant Editor*

Image Credits

All images from iStock and Shutterstock.

Standards

© Copyright 2010. National Governors Association Center for Best Practices and Council of Chief State School Officers. All rights reserved.
© Copyright 2007–2015 Texas Education Association (TEA). All rights reserved.

Shell Education
A division of Teacher Created Materials
5301 Oceanus Drive
Huntington Beach, CA 92649-1030

http://www.tcmpub.com/shell-education
ISBN 978-1-4258-1654-4
©2017 Shell Education Publishing, Inc.

Table of Contents

51654—Guided Math Workshop

Foreword

As a young teacher, I grew up in the tradition of *Mathematics Their Way*. Engaging students in hands-on, relevant, engaging mathematics activities permeated my mathematics classroom. Lively learning accompanied by engaged math talk and focused discovery could be witnessed from all perspectives. Math was truly a favorite time of the day for my students.

During Math Centers, students were engaged in actively "inventing" mathematical understanding. Furthermore, they represented their thinking in a plethora of ways—from pictures, to words, to manipulatives, to equations, mathematical thinking was made visible and audible. My philosophy included the notion that when mathematics is taught well, language develops concurrently, a mainstay in my classroom.

Now, as a mathematics leader both in my own community and across the country, I work with hundreds of teachers every year, supporting them as they create classrooms where mathematics teaching and learning are dynamic processes. I am always on the look-out for resources that will help my teachers successfully merge the rich mathematics content they are teaching with instructional strategies and structures that maximize their impact.

I am excited to proclaim that *Guided Math Workshop* is now on my short list of teaching resources I'll be recommending to my colleagues from this point on. I only wish that this resource had been around when I was first putting together my Math Centers. So much of what I had to learn through trial and error is explained clearly and with great detail. Laney and Donna created a masterpiece that includes an abundance of options to ponder as one designs just the right combination of the Guided Math Workshop components.

This practical guidebook provides everything needed for busy educators to bring math to life in their classrooms using the various workshop principles. Within the pages of this book, one finds a variety of teaching strategies, classroom tips, and student tasks that provide everything needed to get Guided Math Workshops up and running.

In addition to student tasks and introductory lessons, this book includes sections on student reflection and accountability, setting up the classroom space, tips for math coaches, running PLCs, selecting the just-right rotation model, and so much more.

Students learn mathematics best when they engage with authentic, real-world mathematics opportunities. Once you've examined these pages, I'm sure you'll agree that *Guided Math Workshop* provides a dynamic, energetic way to ignite students' enthusiasm toward mathematics.

—Kimberly A. Rimbey, Ph.D.
NBCT, Early Adolescent Mathematics
Co-founder and CEO, *KP Mathematics*
Director of Curriculum & Assessment,
Buckeye Elementary School District

Acknowledgments

Writing is both a labor of love and a heavy burden for authors. Each book brings its own challenges—especially in those last few weeks before it is due to the publisher. This book, though, has been a joy to co-write with my friend and treasured colleague, Donna Boucher. The Math Workstation tasks she created for this book mesh so well with my vision of Math Workshop. Not only that, but she has been exceptionally easy to work with. I hope our collaboration has resulted in something that will be a valuable resource for teachers as they implement Math Workshop in their classrooms.

As always, I thank the many teachers whose classrooms I have visited in the past few years. I feel fortunate to have learned from you even as I was sharing my own ideas. We are all in this together. In education, as in raising a child, it truly takes a village.

Thanks are also due to the wonderful editors at Shell Education. It has been a pleasure to work with Paula Makridis and Diana Kenney in preparing this book. Their insights and suggestions that have improved this work are appreciated.

And, what would I do without the support of my family? Thank you to my daughter and son and their families for all their encouragement and interest in something that is not always of much interest to those outside the classroom. Finally, last, but far from least, thank you to my husband, Jack. Even though I know that just one more mention of Guided Math is enough to push him to the edge, he is usually gracious enough to at least appear to listen to me talk about it. For that, I am very grateful.

—Laney Sammons

Acknowledgments

In Laney Sammons I have found a friend, colleague, and mentor. I am grateful for the doors she has opened for me. I am also grateful that we are as likely to talk about baseball as math when we're together. It is that fellowship that makes working with Laney a true pleasure. I am also thankful for the seismic change in math education that has resulted from her original book, *Guided Math*. It was through that book that I came to know and respect Laney. As a teacher, instructional coach, and interventionist, I have experienced the power of the Guided Math framework, and I am supremely honored to be involved with Laney and Shell Education in the making of this resource.

I could not do what I do without the unique and amazing children who pass through my doors on a daily basis. Thanks to them, each and every day is a new learning experience for me, and they drive me to always want to be a better teacher. Natassja, early on you taught me the very important lesson that being a teacher is not just about teaching math or science, and I thank you for that.

An endeavor such as this is made that much sweeter when shared with family and friends. My dad and sister have been sources of constant support, not only with this book but through all the twists and turns of my life. I hope that I have honored my mom's legacy as a strong, independent woman and that she would be proud of my accomplishments. To Sara, my biggest cheerleader, I treasure our special bond and all the "squeal moments" we have shared, from the very first mention of this book to the present. Finally, I thank my amazing son, Chris. He is my most precious creation and the reason I breathe.

—Donna Boucher

The Guided Math Framework

Guided Math (Sammons 2010, 2014) is an instructional framework that helps teachers provide quality mathematics instruction for their students. Teachers address their students' varied learning needs within a carefully planned numeracy-rich environment where students are challenged to not just *do* math, but instead *become* mathematicians. Implemented together, Guided Math's seven components are designed to help students as they develop a deep conceptual understanding of math, acquire computational fluency, and become skilled in thinking and acting mathematically. Teachers target the specific needs of learners with small-group lessons as students work independently on Math Workstation tasks.

Instructional Components of Guided Math:

1. A Classroom Environment of Numeracy

2. Math Warm-Ups

3. Whole-Class Instruction

4. Small-Group Instruction

5. Math Workshop

6. Math Conferences

7. Balanced Assessments

These components offer teachers ways of engaging in research-based best practices to support the mathematical achievement of all students according to their unique needs (Sammons 2010). Figure I.1 provides an overview of each of the seven Guided Math components.

Figure I.1 Guided Math Menu of Instruction

Classroom Environment of Numeracy (Daily)

In this type of classroom environment, students are immersed in math. The classroom contains evidence of real-life math tasks, data analysis, math word walls, instruments of measurement, mathematical communication, class-created math anchor charts, graphic organizers, calendars, and authentic problem-solving challenges.

Math Warm-Ups (Daily)

This daily appetizer prepares students for the "Your Choice" entrees with Math Stretches, calendar activities, problems of the day, math-related classroom responsibilities, data work, incredible equations, reviews of skills to be maintained, and previews of skills to come.

Whole-Class Instruction (Your Choice)

This is an excellent teaching strategy to use when students are working at the same level of achievement, to introduce lessons with an activating strategy, for teacher modeling and think-alouds, for read-alouds of math-related literature, to review previously mastered skills, as preparation for work in cooperative groups, for paper and pencil assessments, or for Math Huddles.

Small-Group Instruction (Your Choice)

Students are instructed in small groups whose composition changes based on their needs. The individualized preparation for these groups offers tantalizing opportunities to introduce new concepts, practice new skills, work with manipulatives, provide intensive and targeted instruction to struggling learners, introduce activities that will later become part of Math Workshop, conduct informal assessments, and reteach based on student needs.

Math Workshop (Your Choice)

Students work independently, either individually, in pairs, or in cooperative groups. The work may be follow-up from whole-class or small-group instruction, ongoing practice of previously mastered skills, investigations, math games, math journals, or interdisciplinary work. It allows teachers to conduct small-group lessons and conferences.

Conferences (Daily)

To enhance learning, teachers confer individually with students, informally assessing understanding, providing opportunities for one-on-one mathematical communication, and determining teaching points for individual students as well as for the class and conduct brief, focused instruction.

Assessment (Daily)

A generous helping of assessment *for* learning to inform instruction with a dollop of assessment *of* learning to top off each unit is essential to determine instructional needs of each student. These assessments are balanced—based not only on work products, but also on observation of students as they work and mathematical conversations with learners.

(Sammons 2010)

What Is Math Workshop?

Math Workshop is a key ingredient of success in a Guided Math classroom (Sammons 2010, 2013). As one of the most versatile components of the framework, it accommodates a vast array of learning tasks. Not only does it provide opportunities for students to learn how to work independently on worthwhile mathematical endeavors, but it also allows teachers to work with small groups or to confer with individual students.

During Math Workshop, students work independently—individually, in pairs, or in groups—and participate in Math Workstation tasks that have been designed to provide ongoing practice of previously mastered concepts and skills, to promote computational fluency, and to encourage mathematical curiosity and inquiry. In the first weeks of school, students learn and repeatedly practice the routines and procedures that make Math Workshop function smoothly. As students assume greater independence for their learning during Math Workshop, teachers may then expand their teaching roles as seen in Figure I.2.

Figure I.2 The Roles of Teachers and Students during Math Workshop

Teachers	Students
• Teach small-group lessons • Conduct math conferences • Informally assess learning through observations • Facilitate mathematical learning and curiosity through questioning	• Assume responsibility for their learning and behavior • Function as fledgling mathematicians • Communicate mathematically with peers • Review and practice previously mastered concepts and skills • Improve computational fluency • Increase ability to work cooperatively with peers

Because of its instructional value to both students and teachers, Math Workshop is an essential component of a Guided Math classroom. This book offers specific guidance for establishing an effective Math Workshop. It includes the following:

➡ practical strategies for implementation

➡ a selection of workshop models

➡ tips for classroom organization

➡ suggestions for management

➡ sample Math Workstation tasks

➡ a guide for the first 15 days

What are Math Workstations?

Workstations are collections of tasks stored together and worked on independently by students in specified workspaces. Students often work in pairs or small groups but may work alone. Each station contains a variety of carefully selected math tasks to support mathematical learning. Some of the tasks may be mandatory, while others may be optional. Essential for an effective Math Workshop is the inclusion of high-quality, appropriate tasks in the workstations. By grappling with these tasks independently, students gain greater mathematical proficiency and confidence in their mathematical abilities. Here, students "practice problem solving while reasoning, representing, communicating, and making connections among mathematical topics as the teacher observes and interacts with individuals at work or meets with a small group for differentiated math instruction" (Diller 2011, 7).

Math Centers versus Math Workstations

For many years, classrooms contained Math Centers where learners worked independently. Math Centers were considerably different from today's Math Workstations. Even the label *Math Workstation* itself clearly sends the message that students are expected to *work* as mathematicians. Workstation tasks are not included for fun alone, but to further students' understanding of math, improve their computational fluency, and increase their mathematical competency. Figure I.3 highlights the differences between Math Centers and Math Workstations.

Figure I.3 Math Centers versus Math Workstations

Math Centers	Math Workstations
• Games and activities are introduced to students when distributed at centers and are rarely used for instructional purposes.	• Tasks are derived from materials previously used during instruction, so students are already familiar with them.
• Centers are often thematic and change weekly.	• Tasks are changed for instructional purposes, not because it is the end of the week.
• Centers are often made available to students after they complete their regular work.	• Tasks provide ongoing practice to help students retain and deepen their understanding and are an important part of students' mathematical instruction.
• All students work on the same centers, and activities are seldom differentiated.	• Tasks are differentiated to meet the identified learning needs of students.

Levels of Instructional Support

The components of the Guided Math framework align well with the gradual release of the instructional responsibility model described by Pearson and Gallagher (1983). Included in this concept of instructional responsibility is the assessment of students' understanding and learning needs, the crafting of questions to spur deeper thinking, and community building.

Instructional responsibilities are not to be confused with the thinking and learning responsibilities placed on students. Learners must have opportunities to productively struggle to understand mathematical meaning. Instead, the responsibility referred to in this section is that of engaging in various instructional structures promoting inquiry-based learning tasks in which students construct meaning. This type of learning may occur as teachers have the primary responsibility for structuring and facilitating the lesson, when the responsibility is shared between teacher and students, or when students work independently.

Whole-class instruction provides full support for students with the primary responsibility falling on the teacher to plan and deliver challenging lessons that activate prior knowledge, provide direct instruction, model mathematical thinking strategies, or facilitate math huddle discussions. While directing instruction, teachers may facilitate math talks, model thinking like a mathematician (as opposed to modeling specific procedures for solving particular types of problems), or direct activities to activate students' prior knowledge.

As students engage in small-group lessons, responsibility is gradually released as the teacher provides only moderate support. Teachers continue to introduce new concepts, respond to students' learning needs, and conduct informal assessments. Students are more actively engaged with the content of the lesson by constructing mathematical meaning. Students and teachers jointly assume responsibility for assessing understanding and proficiency.

Finally, with Math Workshop, teacher support is very limited. Although the teacher plans the Math Workstation tasks, students carry out their mathematical work independently. Students are expected not only to assume the responsibility of completing the assigned Math Workstation tasks but also to self-assess their learning, take steps to clear up any confusion they may have, and determine their progress toward their learning goals.

With the gradual release of responsibility model, teachers use their professional judgment to determine the appropriate level of support to provide based on their knowledge of student needs and the mathematical content to be learned. Figure I.4 provides an overview of the level of instructional support for Guided Math components along with the the roles of teachers and students.

Figure I.4 Levels of Instructional Support

Guided Math Component	Level of Teacher Support	Teacher Role	Student Role
Whole-Class Instruction	Full Support	• Activate prior knowledge • Model mathematical thinking strategies • Facilitate mathematical discourse • Provide limited direct instruction	• Respond to teacher's questions • Discuss and collaborate with peers • Share thinking as a member of a mathematical community
Small-Group Lessons	Moderate Support	• Introduce new concepts • Provide targeted instruction and scaffolds based on student needs • Informally assess student understanding	• Construct mathematical meaning • Practice newly learned skills • Work with manipulatives • Engage in the mathematical practices/processes
Math Workshop	Limited Support	• Establish routines and procedures • Provide purposeful and engaging Math Workstation tasks • Create a system for student accountability	• Practice previously mastered concepts and skills • Strengthen math computational skills to build fluency • Conduct mathematical investigations

(Adapted from Sammons 2013)

Rationale for Math Workshop

For many teachers, the implementation of Math Workshop is one of the most challenging aspects of the Guided Math framework. Teachers are often concerned about how to effectively manage student behavior, how to plan and create worthwhile Math Workstation tasks, and how to hold students accountable for their work. They may also fear giving up the control they experience with whole-class instruction. Some primary-grade teachers may worry their students are too young to work independently. Upper elementary and middle school teachers may worry their students will be distracted or influenced negatively by peer pressure. Yet, across all of these grade levels, teachers are discovering that Math Workshop undeniably enhances their mathematics instruction. So, why do they find it to be so valuable?

➡ **Math Workshop promotes student independence and self-reliance.** Teachers have the responsibility of doing more than just imparting information. Educators are tasked with empowering "students so they will be self-guided, confident, autonomous, lifelong learners and achievers…. In order for our students to gain the control those qualities require, we have to give some of our control away. We have to relinquish the center of the stage and hang out in the periphery while students work cooperatively, teach each other, and make choices that guide their actions" (Koenig 2010, 25). The learning environment established in Math Workshop is one in which students have opportunities to do just that.

➡ **Math Workshop allows teachers time to conduct small-group lessons and math conferences that specifically target students' learning needs.** In traditional classrooms, teachers are front and center throughout the day—either directly instructing students or closely supervising their practice. With that instructional model, when can teachers meet with small groups or individual students? Unless students are capable of working independently and are productively engaged, these highly focused and effective teaching formats are impossible for teachers to provide.

➡ **Math Workshop provides ample opportunity for ongoing practice of previously mastered concepts and skills (distributed practice).** There never seems to be enough time for the practice of previously mastered concepts and skills. With demanding curricula to be learned by students within just one academic year, teachers often feel the need to move from one unit to the next with little time for ongoing practice to maintain and deepen mathematical understanding. And then, all too often, lengthy and intensive review sessions precede standardized testing supplanting instructional time that might have been used to teach new content.

According to Goodwin (2014), "not all practice is created equal" (77). While *massed* practice—initial practice sessions grouped together—is useful for developing automaticity, it is crucial that students have opportunities for *distributed* practice—repeated practice sessions scheduled over a period of time—for long-term retention. Revisiting previously learned concepts and skills reinforces neural pathways in the brain and moves the information or skill into students' permanent memories.

Math Workshop is an ideal time to assign distributed practice as Math Workstation tasks. These are tasks students should be able to complete independently and with accuracy. Revisiting previously mastered concepts and skills helps students retain what they have learned and leads to deeper understanding.

➡ **Math Workshop delivers valuable time for students to improve their computational fluency.** Computational fluency is more than just the memorization of math facts and is, in fact, something distinct from automaticity (Bay-Williams and Kling 2014). Fluency demands students are efficient, accurate, and flexible when solving problems. Emphasizing both skill and understanding, teachers may help students move beyond simply memorizing facts to develop a *mathematical memory* in which their understanding of mathematical procedures is grounded in a web of interconnected mathematical concepts and relationships (Russell 2000). When students recognize the meaning behind procedures, they are much more likely to remember and apply them appropriately in other contexts.

To acquire computational fluency, students need *many* and *varied* opportunities for meaningful and engaging practice. Tasks requiring students to solve story problems or to work with manipulatives to increase number sense may become Math Workstation tasks. Games offer valuable alternatives to worksheets in supporting the development of fluency. The inclusion of games as part of independent work during Math Workshop makes fluency practice not only educational but also fun. These types of tasks are well suited for Math Workstations, since students may work on them independently.

➡ **Math Workshop allows time for students to engage in the mathematical practices or processes embedded in Math Workstation tasks.** The Standards for Mathematical Practice set forth in the Common Core Mathematics State Standards "describe varieties of expertise that mathematics educators at all levels should seek to develop in their students" (NGA and CCSSO 2010, 6). This document emphasizes the "need to connect the mathematical practices to mathematical content in mathematics instruction" (8). The process standards included in the Texas Essential Knowledge and Skills for Mathematics "describe ways in which students are expected to engage in the content" to enable them to "be successful problem-solvers and use mathematics efficiently and effectively in daily life." (Texas Education Agency, 2012) Carefully designed Math Workstation tasks strengthen students' abilities in the essential mathematical processes and proficiencies.

➡ **Math Workshop offers opportunities to differentiate instruction based on students' learning needs.** Math Workstations can be differentiated to meet students' diverse learning needs. Some tasks allow for self-differentiation options, such as giving students control over the difficulty level of problems, providing number stories in which students create questions, offering open-ended probes, or by encouraging students to show their understanding in different ways (Dacey and Salemi 2007). In addition, teachers may differentiate by assigning parallel tasks—usually two or three that "get at the same big idea and are close enough in context that they can be discussed simultaneously" (Small 2012, 10), but which vary to meet the diverse learning needs of students. For example, tasks might differ as to the operations being performed or the magnitude of the numbers involved in the tasks.

➡ **Math Workshop promotes mathematical discourse among students.** As students work independently in pairs or small groups, they share their mathematical thinking. These conversations promote thinking, build a sense of community, and lead to greater metacognition (Hoffer 2012). Of course, mathematical discourse skills must be taught first, but the workshop structure and scaffolding provided by Talking Points cards (see chapter 2) provide ongoing practice of these skills.

➡ **Math Workshop enhances students' ability to work collaboratively and cooperatively.** According to the National Education Association's report Preparing 21st Century Students for a Global Society, "collaboration is essential in our classrooms because it is inherent in the nature of how work is accomplished in our civic and workforce lives" (National Education Association 2012, 16). During Math Workshop, students learn to work respectfully with others, exercise flexibility and willingness to work toward a common goal, and assume responsibility for shared work products. As Hoffer (2012, 5) explains, students "build confidence and competence as members of a community of mathematicians."

In addition to building these important life skills, research shows that the types of collaborative work done in Math Workshop enhances the achievement of students. As a result of his synthesis of recent educational research, Hattie (2009) found that cooperative work had a medium to high effect on learning as compared to more individualized learning activities.

➡ **Math Workshop enables students to work on mathematical investigations and to pursue their curiosity about mathematics.** During Math Workshop, students have opportunities to *really* act as mathematicians—going beyond worksheets and textbook assignments. They begin to more fully appreciate the discipline, as they are encouraged to wonder about how math relates to the world around them. Because of the independent nature of Math Workshop, a student who is an avid sports fan might do a statistical analysis of an aspect of a sport. A student who wonders about weather patterns might investigate current climate trends. A young politico might work with data from polling to make election predictions. Or, a budding investment banker might engage in a stock market analysis or an investment game. And, as they investigate and pursue their curiosity, they are discovering the relevance of mathematics in the real world.

➡ **Math Workshop offers the flexibility needed for unconventional mathematical tasks.** Students may also interact with mathematics in unconventional ways in workstations. They might create books or slideshow presentations explaining mathematical concepts. They might be challenged to solve a school-wide problem (e.g., studying the traffic patterns in the halls to solve congestion issues). They might be asked to figure out the most efficient way to set up chairs for a large group meeting. Or, they might be involved in planning a math night event for a school open house. These kinds of tasks require students to consider many factors and diverse aspects of practical problem solving—the kind of work that mathematicians do in the real world.

Getting Started

This resource will guide you through the implementation process of Math Workshop by offering effective strategies and options for you to consider. The following is an overview of the chapters in this book and exploratory questions that are addressed in each chapter.

Chapter 1: Structuring Math Workshop gives an overview of a variety of workshop models that teachers may use. It offers suggestions as to what you should take into consideration when choosing a workshop model, as well as suggestions for workstation management boards. This chapter provides answers for these questions:

1. What Math Workshop model will work best for me?

2. How can I create a management board to help students identify where they will work during Math Workshop?

Chapter 2: Organizing Math Workshop offers guidance for classroom arrangements conducive to Math Workshop, organization of mathematics materials, and preparation for an effective Math Workshop. This chapter gives suggestions for the mechanics of creating Math Workstation tasks that help students work independently. It answers the following questions:

1. How can I arrange my classroom to effectively accommodate Math Workstations?

2. What should I include in Math Workstations?

Chapter 3: Managing Math Workshop provides strategies for developing effective routines and procedures for Math Workshop. Methods of holding students accountable for their independent work are explored. In addition, the chapter examines support that you may draw upon by working with coaches or with Professional Learning Communities as you implement Math Workshop. It answers the following questions:

1. What should I take into consideration as I develop routines and procedures for students working independently in Math Workshop?

2. How will I hold students accountable for their independent work during Math Workshop?

Chapter 4: Planning Math Workstations focuses on grouping students for effective independent work during Math Workshop and creating engaging and worthwhile Math Workstation tasks. Suggestions for the use of digital devices are also provided. This chapter addresses the following questions:

1. How should I group students during Math Workshop?

2. What kinds of tasks should I include in Math Workstations?

3. How can I incorporate the use of digital devices into Math Workshop?

Chapter 5: Math Workstation Tasks is a compilation of sample tasks grouped by grade-level bands (e.g., K–2, 3–5, 6–8) that may be easily adapted for use in other grade levels. Each task includes an overview page, a Student Task card, and a Talking Points card in this chapter. The additional resources for each task may be found in Appendix C. The following questions are addressed in this chapter:

1. What kinds of tasks are best for Math Workstations?

2. How can I differentiate workstation tasks for my students?

3. In what ways can I hold students accountable for their independent work on a Math Workstation task?

Chapter 6: Implementing Math Workshop gives you guidance on how to introduce and teach the routines and procedures your students will need to know. It describes how to plan lessons and provide practice for students during the first 15 days of Math Workshop. The chapter also addresses strategies for introducing new Math Workstation tasks to your students to ensure that they have a good understanding of the tasks and their responsibilities as they work independently. Sample lessons illustrate the use of these strategies. Refer to this chapter to answer these questions:

1. What is the best way to teach students workshop routines and procedures?

2. How should I introduce new Math Workstation tasks to students?

Chapter 7: Your Turn! gives you a place to brainstorm and plan what Math Workshop will look like in your classroom. This chapter explores these questions:

1. Which Math Workshop rotation model will I use in my classroom and why?

2. What routines and procedures are important for my students to know in Math Workshop?

3. What tasks will I include in Math Workstations?

Digital resources to support the workstation tasks in this book are available online. A complete list of available documents is provided on pages 228–231. To access the digital resources, go to this website: **http://www.tcmpub.com/download-files**. Enter this code: 35961528. Follow the on-screen directions.

Structuring Math Workshop

As you create a plan for implementing Math Workshop, remember that Math Workshop structures are extremely flexible. Teachers may be able to use a variety of workshop models effectively. Explore the options, and decide which is best for your classroom. Each workshop model has its unique advantages and disadvantages. Your decision of which model to use is not irreversible.

Consider the following as you evaluate each Math Workshop model when choosing the best option for your class:

➡ Amount of student movement required

➡ Degree of flexibility for conducting small-group lessons

➡ Likely noise level

➡ Volunteer or staff support available to you

➡ Amount of planning required

➡ Space available in your classroom

➡ Your classroom management style

➡ Amount of technology available for student use

How Much Choice Will Students Have?

Allowing students some degree of choice has a positive effect on students' general well being, their behavior and values, and their academic achievement (Kohn 1993). The amount of freedom given to students varies from teacher to teacher. Some teachers are comfortable offering their students more instructional options than others. With Math Workshop, you decide how much choice to offer your students. Here are some questions to consider when deciding how much choice students will have during Math Workshop:

➡ Will workstations be assigned, or will students be able to choose?

➡ With whom will students work? Will you assign students to work individually or with other students? Or, will students choose their partners?

➡ Which tasks will be completed? Are all tasks compulsory? Or, are some tasks optional?

➡ What methods will students use to complete tasks? (e.g., journal entries, creation of digital slideshows, audio recordings, physical models)

➡ What materials will students use to complete tasks? (e.g., base-ten blocks, virtual manipulatives, diagrams, number cards)

➡ May students visit more than one Math Workstation during a given time period? May students move from one station to another if they complete their work? What if they would rather work at another station?

As you make decisions regarding student choice, consider your own classroom management style, your students and their work habits, and your vision for an effective Math Workshop. Keep in mind that if you offer choices to students, teaching them how to responsibly make choices must be a part of teaching routines and procedures. If you are unsure about how much choice to allow students, try it out. Offer students a choice to see how well it works. If students respond well, offer more choices.

Will Students Work Individually, in Pairs, or in Small Groups?

In making this determination, it is important to recognize the fact that the larger the group working together, the greater the noise level and the greater the chance they will drift off task. Yet, that is only one factor to consider when making this decision.

Mathematics learning, at its best, is a social process (Sammons 2010, 2013). While students working individually may work quietly, they need opportunities to learn how to collaborate with their peers, to share their mathematical thinking with others, and to learn from their fellow mathematicians (Vygotsky 1978). Moreover, mathematics learning increases as students work collaboratively tackling new math concepts and skills (Van de Walle and Lovin 2006). When students work together in pairs or small groups, the classroom truly becomes a mathematical learning community with students sharing ideas and talking collectively about math. The reflective conversations that result lead young mathematicians to fully engage with the ideas of others—constructing hypotheses, considering strategies, and understanding concepts (Nichols 2006).

When deciding how students will work during Math Workshop, you may choose different structures for how students work. Even when groups rotate to workstations together, teachers may choose to have them complete tasks individually or in pairs. Although there are advantages to having students engage individually in independent work at times, it is advisable to provide ample opportunity for students to work closely with other learners—either in pairs or in small groups.

Selecting a Math Workshop Model

Rotation Models for Groups

The most common Math Workshop model is based on the rotation of small groups of students from workstation to workstation on a regular schedule. Each group works at each workstation every day. If there are three workstations and the Math Workshop time block is one hour, groups rotate every 20 minutes. With four workstations, groups rotate every 15 minutes. Or, an alternative may be to have the workstation materials rotated from group to group on that schedule. Although this is not commonly done, it is an option that minimizes student movement.

A teacher workstation is included in many rotational models, where the teacher facilitates a small-group lesson as one of the daily workstations. Students are grouped homogeneously so that the teacher may differentiate the lesson based on their similar learning needs. Of course, effective differentiation occurs only when student groupings are flexible and change from day to day based on that day's lesson. The fluidity of the groupings means the class is not simply divided into a low group, a medium group, and a high group. Instead, teachers use assessment data, both formal and informal, to determine instructional groups so that gaps in understanding and skill may be filled and additional challenge provided when appropriate. Figure 1.1 shows examples of rotational models with the small-group lesson as a workstation.

Figure 1.1 Workstation Rotation Models with Teacher Station

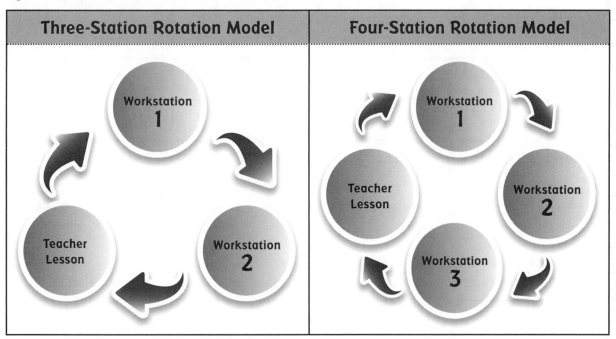

A workstation management board ensures students know where they will work and time is not wasted during transitions. A management board may be created for three or four homogeneous groups of students in which the teacher lesson is part of the rotation, as shown in Figure 1.2 and Figure 1.3.

Figure 1.2 Sample Management Board for Three Workstations with Teacher Station

Red Team Tom, Carlos, Jasmine, Min, Sadie, and Assad	Blue Team Finn, Sandra, Fatima, Maria, Joseph, and Lois	Yellow Team Sara, Pedro, Mimi, Matt, Krista, and Ravi
Teacher Station	Workstation 2	Workstation 1
Workstation 1	Teacher Station	Workstation 2
Workstation 2	Workstation 1	Teacher Station

Figure 1.3 Sample Management Board for Four Workstations with Teacher Station

Red Team Tom, Carlos, Jasmine, Min, Sadie, and Assad	Blue Team Finn, Sandra, Fatima, Maria, Joseph, and Lois	Yellow Team Sara, Pedro, Mimi, Matt, Krista, and Ravi	Green Team Ash, Dempsey, Griff, Alice, Yoshi, and Carmen
Workstation 1	Teacher Station	Workstation 3	Workstation 2
Workstation 2	Workstation 1	Teacher Station	Workstation 3
Workstation 3	Workstation 2	Workstation 1	Teacher Station
Teacher Station	Workstation 3	Workstation 2	Workstation 1

In other rotation models, groups of students rotate on a set schedule that does not include a teacher lesson. Instead, the teacher pulls students on an as-needed basis for lessons. While this model is more complex, it provides a greater degree of flexibility for small-group lessons.

The composition of the rotating groups may be heterogeneous, if desired, but for small-group lessons, the groups are homogeneous so that the unique learning needs of the students are targeted. With this model, not only does the composition of the groups vary according to the lesson, but the length of the lessons may also differ depending on the instructional needs of the groups. Throughout the workstation period, the heterogeneous groups continue to rotate to the workstations on a regular schedule while the teacher calls small groups for lessons as needed. Figure 1.4 shows examples of rotational models when the teacher lesson is not one of the workstations.

Figure 1.4 Workstation Rotation Models without Teacher Station

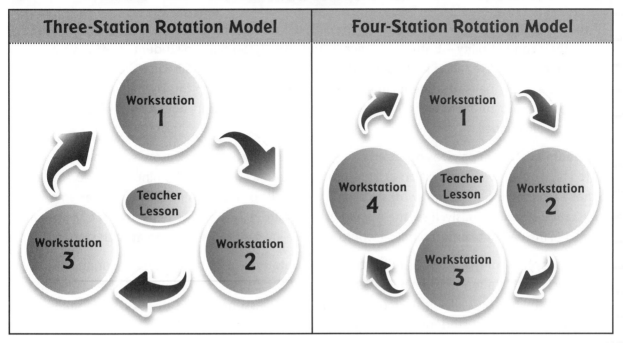

You may create Math Workstation management boards to indicate where students will work during Math Workshop for a rotation model without a teacher station. An example is shown in Figure 1.5.

Figure 1.5 Sample Management Board for Four Workstations without Teacher Station

Red Team Tom, Carlos, Jasmine, Min, Sadie, and Assad	Blue Team Finn, Sandra, Fatima, Maria, Joseph, and Lois	Yellow Team Sara, Pedro, Mimi, Matt, Krista, and Ravi	Green Team Ash, Dempsey, Griff, Alice, Yoshi, and Carmen
Workstation 1	Workstation 4	Workstation 3	Workstation 2
Workstation 2	Workstation 1	Workstation 4	Workstation 3
Workstation 3	Workstation 2	Workstation 1	Workstation 4
Workstation 4	Workstation 3	Workstation 2	Workstation 1

Rotation Models for Pairs of Students

If you prefer to have your students work in pairs, it is best that you assign pairs of students to ensure their compatibility—both academically and socially. So that no student is left to work alone when groups are called for lessons, students in each pair should be in the same instructional groups. As a result, pairs of students may have the same needs. With this model, students do not have the opportunity to work on workstation tasks with students who have a range of mathematical abilities.

Students working in pairs, as opposed to larger groups, tend to speak more softly and are more apt to stay engaged in workstation tasks. This model usually requires planning more workstations so that each pair has a different workstation. Several pairs of students may work at the same workstation simultaneously. If so, the management board may look much like the one shown in Figure 1.5. Instead of teams, the board would indicate student pairs working at each station.

Another option for this model is to have only two rotations of 30 minutes each during an hour math block. Each station would have several tasks for the pairs to complete. As the pairs work at stations, the teacher calls up students for small-group lessons. Figure 1.6 shows a sample management board for students working in pairs.

Figure 1.6 Sample Management Board for Student Pairs

Students		First Workstation	Second Workstation
Anuska	Michael	1	2
Tito	Meg	2	3
Chika	Juan	3	4
Skyler	Marta	4	5
Dylan	Shiro	5	1

(Sammons 2013, 226)

Multiple Workstations with Student Choice

Another Math Workshop model often used by teachers is one in which students choose from each day. It is very important that the management board clearly indicates where students may work. Valuable instructional time may be lost if students are confused and need to be redirected.

According to Diller (2011), choice plays an important role in the success of Math Workstations, and this model offers an effective way of providing choice. She cautions, however, that too many choices may overwhelm students. Teachers should offer *controlled choice*, especially at the beginning of the school year. Sometimes, choice is limited because the teacher requires certain workstation tasks to be completed each week. If you choose this model and require students to complete particular workstation tasks, help students develop responsibility for monitoring their work by providing checklists to show what they have completed and what still needs to be done. A sample checklist is shown in Figure 1.7.

Figure 1.7 Sample Checklist for Multiple Workstations with Student Choice

Name: _____ Date: _____

Math Workstations Checklist

Directions: Complete at least five workstations during the week. Draw an X next to the workstation when you have completed the task.

- ☐ Workstation 1: Math Literature
- ☐ Workstation 2: Computational Fluency
- ☐ Workstation 3: Problem Solving
- ☐ Workstation 4: Place Value
- ☐ Workstation 5: Measurement Practice
- ☐ Workstation 6: Math Vocabulary

With this model, workstations may either be named or given a number. Numbering stations makes management boards simpler because materials or content of the stations may be changed without having to change workstation labels. Workstation 1 may include tasks in which students are engaged in number sense activities one week but geometry the next.

If you decide to have students choose where to work, provide clear guidelines regarding how the workshop structure operates. Establish how many students may participate in each workstation at a time, and devise a way of letting students know when the stations are full.

One option for primary-grade students might be to attach color-coded clothespins that match each workstation to a workstation management board, as shown in Figure 1.8. The colored clothespins indicate the number of students the corresponding station can accommodate. When a student chooses a station, he or she takes a clothespin of the station of his or her choice from the board and attaches it to his or her clothing. If there are no clothespins of that color on the board, it means the workstation is full and the student must choose another workstation.

Figure 1.8 Sample Workstation Choice Management Board with Clothespins

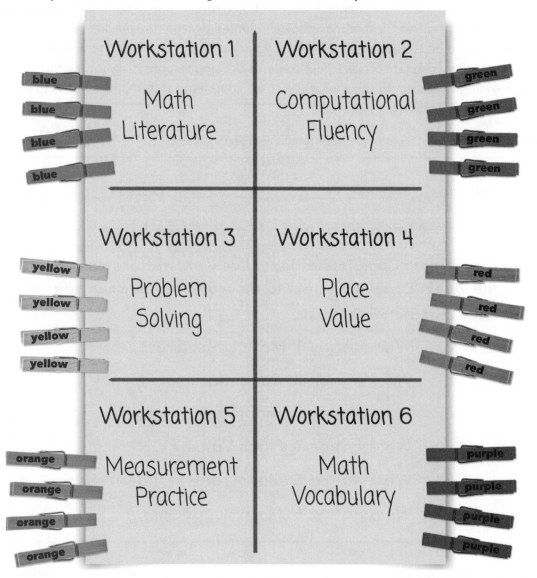

Another option for a management board is to have Velcro® dots that indicate how many students may work at each workstation, as shown in Figure 1.9. In this option, each student has a Velcro®-backed gingerbread figure with his or her name on it. Students place their figures on the Velcro® dots for workstations. If all the dots for a station are already filled, students must choose other workstations.

Figure 1.9 Sample Workstation Choice Management Board with Velcro® Dots

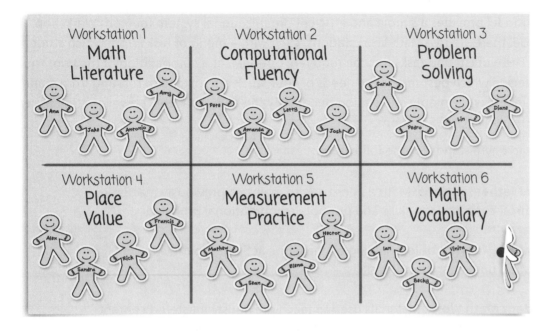

For upper-grade students, you may want to use a pocket chart to help students indicate workstation choice. In this option, each row on the chart has a card labeled with the workstation number and task and indicates the number of students who may work at the station at a time. Students will place their name cards in the rows of the stations where they choose to work. A sample pocket chart is shown in Figure 1.10.

Figure 1.10 Sample Workstation Choice Management Board with a Pocket Chart

Workstation 1	Math Literature (6 max)	Jasmine	Ennis	Jiro	Ashia	Tonya	Raj
Workstation 2	Computational Fluency (4 max)	Patricio	Christy	Megan	Jamar		
Workstation 3	Problem Solving (4 max)	Keke	Hua	Finn	Amanda		
Workstation 4	Place Value (4 max)	Sadie	Scott	Jibri	Thomas		
Workstation 5	Measurement (4 max)	Jacob	Kayla	Mason	Miguel		
Workstation 6	Math Vocabulary (5 max)	Emanuel	Allie	Vincent	Brittany	Omar	

There are many management boards that may be easily adapted for multiple workstation models. If you decide to make choice available to your students during Math Workshop, consider the options just described, but also check with teachers using Math Workshop in your school or district to see what kind of management system they use. Consider what might work for you, and then adapt it to make it your own.

The GUIDE Model

The GUIDE model provides a simple and efficient organizational system for Math Workshop. With this model there are five Math Workstations, each with a menu of tasks from which students may choose. The workstation tasks may be required, optional, or a combination of the two. You as the teacher decide which best meets the needs of your students. Instead of rotating from station to station, students work in only one station per day. By the end of a week, however, students will have worked in all five GUIDE stations.

The GUIDE acronym stands for the following:

Games for Mathematicians: Math games used to maintain previously mastered mathematical concepts and skills and promote computational proficiency

Using What We Know: Problem solving or challenge activities to draw upon mathematical understanding and skills

Independent Math Work: Materials used to teach previously mastered content incorporated into workstation tasks (paper-and-pencil tasks may be included)

Developing Fluency: Tasks that help students develop number sense and mental math skills

Expressing Mathematical Ideas: Mathematical vocabulary and communication are the focus (math journals or math vocabulary notebooks may be included)

Students may be given the choice of where they will work each day, or the teacher may make team assignments. If you allow your students to choose their stations, provide a weekly checklist to track completed stations. Using the checklist, they can clearly see which stations they still need to complete by the end of the week.

This model offers maximum flexibility to teachers. Not only can the composition of small-group lessons be changed at a moment's notice to respond to newly identified student needs, but the length of the lessons may also vary from group to group. Teachers also appreciate another aspect of the flexibility this model offers. If the Math Workshop schedule is interrupted for some reason (e.g., testing day, holiday, whole-group lesson), the rotation schedule simply continues the next day as Math Workshop resumes. So, if a student does *G* on Monday, *U* on Tuesday, and then there is no workshop on Wednesday, he or she would do *I* on Thursday. As a result, students might not do all five workstations in one week, but they would still get to do them all after five Math Workshop days.

A sample GUIDE management board is shown in Figure 1.11. The chart remains the same throughout the week, with only the team assignments changing daily.

Figure 1.11 Sample GUIDE Management Board

G Games for Mathematicians	U Using What We Know	I Independent Math Work	D Developing Fluency	E Expressing Mathematical Ideas
• On a Roll • Math Concentration: Problem Solving • Area and Perimeter War • tablet apps	• $1,000 House • Choose Sides • Read a Book, Write a Problem	• Greatest and Least • problems 1-5 in the textbook • Follow the Rule • Measurement Conversion Board	• Math 24 • tablet apps • Multiples Tic-Tac-Toe • A Matter of Facts	• Wanted Vocabulary Poster • This Reminds Me Of... • Problem-Solving Organizer • Let's Compare
Red Team	Blue Team	Yellow Team	Green Team	Orange Team

(Sammons 2013)

Math Workshop Model Comparison

The models described have all been implemented successfully in Guided Math classrooms, often with adaptions by teachers. The chart in Figure 1.12 can be used to compare and contrast the characteristics of each of these models to help you decide which will work best for you and your class.

Figure 1.12 A Comparison of Math Workshop Models

	Rotation Model with Teacher Lesson Station	Rotation Model without Teacher Lesson Station	Multiple Workstations with Student Choice	GUIDE
Frequency of Models	• each station every day	• each station every day	• students choose workstations (some may be required)	• each station once a week
Number of Workstations	• three to four	• three to four	• multiple	• five
Task Time Required	• 15–20 minutes	• 15–20 minutes	• times vary	• entire Math Workshop block
Task Type	• compulsory and/or choice tasks	• compulsory and/or choice tasks	• choice tasks, some may be compulsory	• compulsory and/or choice tasks
Frequency of Task Changes	• daily or weekly	• daily or weekly	• usually weekly, but at teacher's discretion	• only when appropriate
Student Rotation	• between stations at set times	• between stations at set times	• by choice	• remain in one workstation
Grouping of Students	• homogeneous	• heterogeneous	• heterogeneous	• heterogeneous
Small-Group Lessons	• teacher leads with each group rotating daily	• teacher leads with homogeneous groups	• teacher leads with homogeneous groups	• teacher leads with homogeneous groups
Lesson Length	• same amount of time for each small-group lesson	• vary according to need	• vary according to need	• vary according to need

While you have a great deal of flexibility in designing a Math Workshop structure for your classroom, it is best to keep the model consistent throughout the year, if possible. Although you might try different models from year to year, it is advisable to remain with one model during the year unless you encounter major problems. Creating and teaching students routines and procedures for Math Workshop is time consuming. Teaching new routines and procedures for a newly adopted workshop model wastes valuable instructional time.

Using This Resource

This book focuses on implementing the GUIDE model for Math Workshop. Strategies are suggested for implementation, organization, management, and use of technology. Additionally, Math Workstation tasks for grade-level bands (e.g., K–2, 3–5, and 6–8) are provided. All of these resources may be adapted and used with *any* of the models described in this chapter. As a teacher, use your professional judgment to decide which model will work best for your class, and then draw upon these resources to support it.

Review and Reflect

1. Have you tried to create a Math Workshop in your classroom? What model did you use? What aspects of it worked well for you? Did you encounter any problems? How did you resolve them?

2. Consider your teaching style and classroom preferences. Taking these into consideration, which model do you think is best for your Guided Math classroom?

Organizing Math Workshop

The organization of Math Workshop can make or break a classroom. Having a well-organized room helps the planning and preparation of workstation tasks flow smoothly, and it also fosters an environment conducive to learning. In fact, one of the foundational principles of Guided Math highlights its importance: "An organized classroom environment supports the learning process" (Sammons 2010, 36). In a well-managed classroom, much thought is given to how to best organize student workspaces and materials to create a productive learning climate for Math Workshop.

Consider these aspects of the organization of your classroom as you implement Math Workshop: classroom arrangement, storage of materials, workstation containers, workstation locations, and creation of a workshop climate that promotes learning.

Strategies for Classroom Arrangement

The arrangement of your classroom significantly impacts the Math Workshop learning environment. A well-arranged room enhances learning and positively affects student behavior (Diller 2016).

As the school year begins, take time to consider your room arrangement. Remember, however, that your classroom arrangement at the beginning of the year is not set in stone. At times throughout the year, continue to reflect on it and assess how well it works during Math Workshop. Do not hesitate to rearrange your classroom based on your experiences as students work independently.

When choosing a classroom arrangement, keep these ideas in mind:

➡ **Designate workstation areas that can accommodate groups of different sizes.** During Math Workshop, students may work individually, in pairs, or in small groups. As you decide where workstations will be located, you may match tasks to spaces that best accommodate the grouping required.

➡ **Establish specific areas for different kinds of work in which students will be engaged—whether it be independent Math Workstation tasks, games, or small-group lessons.** Some spaces are more conducive to specific tasks. For instance, a game might be easily played on a carpeted area of the floor. Or, a group of students creating a poster may need a large table that's close to art supplies. Or, a math literature workstation might be located near the math alcove that houses a collection of math books. Additionally, plan to have an area where a disruptive student may work without disturbing the work of others, if needed.

➡ **Create an area where you can teach small-group lessons without being interrupted by the work of other students.** This area should include space for storing the lesson materials. The small-group lesson area should also have ample space for students to work with manipulatives, yet be small enough that you may closely observe their work and listen to their math talk. When you work with students in this area, you should have a clear view of the classroom and all workstations. Additionally, to prevent students in small-group lessons from being distracted by students working independently, plan to have them seated facing away from other workstation areas whenever possible.

➡ **Think about how to arrange your classroom to accommodate varying levels of noise.** Some workstation tasks encourage more student interaction than others. Consider placing those workstations in areas where interruptions are less likely to occur. Additionally, provide quiet areas for students who work best in calmer settings or for tasks that require quiet concentration.

➡ **Make math materials readily available to students.** Some materials that students need for tasks will be stowed in workstation bins. At times, though, students may require additional materials (e.g., math manipulatives, paper, calculators, or other forms of technology). These items should be stored so that students may easily access them as they work. Low shelves are ideal for younger learners. Housing necessary supplies in low-traffic areas makes retrieval by students go more smoothly. By making materials accessible, teachers promote the development of independent learners who may work productively without interrupting small-group lessons.

➡ **Consider traffic flow of students during Math Workshop.** Arrange your classroom so that traffic moves smoothly during transitions and as students are engaged in workstation tasks. Keep high-traffic areas open and clear. If classroom furniture and other objects are placed too closely together, it may be difficult for students to move around the classroom for transitions or to obtain needed materials without disturbing others.

➡ **Arrange your classroom so that it aligns with your tolerance of student activity.** Some teachers are more comfortable with purposeful student movement than others. Take that into consideration as you plan where materials will be stored and where groups will work.

Keeping the above-mentioned points in mind, plan how you will arrange your room on paper first. Situate taller classroom furnishings against the wall, so you will have a clear view of your students during Math Workshop. Carefully assess the usefulness of furniture in your room. Remove any furnishings that do not serve a purpose to provide more space for students during Math Workshop.

Use the furniture that you have creatively. Can pieces of furniture be used for more than one purpose? Can student desks be pushed together to form tables for workstations? Can an area rug be defined as a workspace? Can dry-erase boards be hung on the back of a low bookcase for students to use as a workstation? Think outside the box to make the most of your classroom furnishings and resources.

Consult with fellow teachers to see what has worked well for them. As you plan, try to eliminate clutter. A cluttered classroom often exacerbates behavior problems (Diller 2016). Get rid of any materials you do not need, and store what is not currently in use somewhere out of sight. The goal is to have a highly functional classroom arrangement that supports independent student work and encourages students to assume responsibility for both their learning and their behavior.

Figure 2.1 shows a sample room arrangement for Math Workshop with a large-group area. A sample room arrangement in a smaller classroom without an area for large-group work is shown in Figure 2.2. Although these arrangements include individual student desks, they work equally as well for classrooms in which students sit at tables. Both of these arrangements include an area for small-group lessons and many areas for independent work. Students may work individually or in groups at the desks that are pushed together, or they may work at tables, at the computers, at the interactive whiteboard, in the math alcove, or on the floor in the large-group area. Materials that students access during Math Workshop may be stored on shelves or in the math alcove. In both of these sample classroom arrangements, the teacher has an unobstructed view of the entire classroom, making workshop management easier. Note that the table for small-group lessons is situated so that most of the students are seated facing away from the workstations. This minimizes distractions caused by students working independently at workstations.

Figure 2.1 Sample Room Arrangement with a Large-Group Area

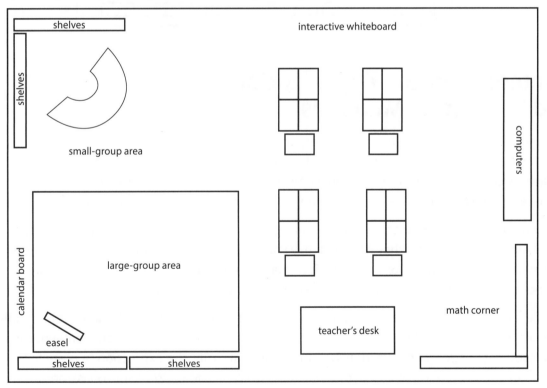

Figure 2.2 Sample Room Arrangement Without a Large-Group Area

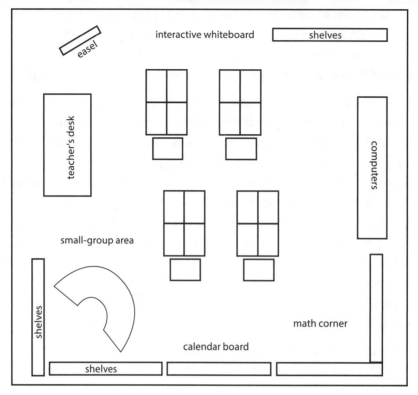

Strategies for the Organization and Storage of Materials

Teachers always appreciate having a variety of mathematics materials to use for instruction in their classrooms. Numerous resources find their way into classrooms and are saved over the years as teachers collect items from professional development opportunities, textbook adoptions, purchases by the central office or school, and personal purchases (Sammons 2013).

Having a wealth of mathematics instructional resources is only of value, however, when teachers know exactly what materials they have and may readily access what they need when they need them. According to Diller (2016), well-organized materials help teachers plan for instruction. "When you know *what* you have to teach with, it makes it easier to think about *how* you teach" (27).

So, as you plan for the implementation of Math Workshop, it is important that your instructional materials be easily accessible—not hidden away in a closet or forgotten. To efficiently use your math resources, a strong organization system is essential. Truly, the expression "a place for everything and everything in its place" is particularly apt in a Math Workshop classroom.

To make your mathematics resources more accessible and to rid your classroom of those you will never use, follow organization guru Julie Morgenstern's (2004) process, SPACE—an acronym for *Sort*, *Purge*, *Assign a Home*, *Containerize*, and *Equalize*.

1. **Sort** your math instructional items. Identify what is important for instruction and what is not. Of those items that are important, categorize them by math domain (e.g., counting and cardinality, number and operations, statistics and probability, geometry, measurement and data, and algebra).

2. **Purge** the materials that are deemed not important to instruction. A word of caution—be aware that some of these materials may belong to your school or district. If there is an inventory of math materials that should be maintained in your classroom, check it carefully. Do not discard any of these without permission from your school (Diller 2011). If you are discarding materials that belong to you, consider offering them to other teachers in your building before disposing of them.

3. **Assign a home** for your mathematics resources. Take into consideration how frequently they will be used. Also, consider whether students will need ready access to them. Locate areas to store them in your classroom where they are available when needed for instruction.

4. **Containerize** and store like items together to make it easy to find what you need when you need it. Use containers that are appropriately sized for the items you are storing. Oversized containers waste valuable storage space. Clearly label each container to indicate its contents, so that it may be easily seen at a glance to facilitate the retrieval of needed materials (Diller 2011). For containers of manipulatives, also label the area where each container is to be kept. To minimize disruption of small-group lessons when students need access to materials, store these containers near areas where students work independently and away from small-group areas whenever possible (Sammons 2010).

5. **Equalize** by continuing to assess and revise your storage system as needed with materials shared out in their appropriate places. Once your storage system is established, consistently maintain it. If you return materials to their "homes" each day, it is much easier to avoid a buildup of clutter and misplaced items. Teach students how to neatly clean their workspaces and put away any materials they use, and then consistently require them to do so. This makes cleanup easier for all and teaches your students valuable organizational life skills.

For teachers whose built-in storage space is limited, the task of organizing and storing materials may be challenging. Various kinds of shelving, stacking cubes, baskets, bins, and portable drawers are commercially available. Many teachers create attractive and functional storage spaces using these kinds of products. Be creative in making use of the space you have in your classroom—especially spaces that may be easily accessed. Rather than stowing materials on top of tall cabinets or closets where they are difficult to reach, store containers in spaces under tables. Attach fabric skirts to the edges of tables so that resources may be hidden, yet are easy to retrieve when needed.

Strategies for Preparing Math Workstations

The following suggestions for preparing workstations are based on the GUIDE model, but they may be easily adapted to support any of the other workshop models described in Chapter 1.

Workstation Containers

Before implementing Math Workshop, take time to plan how workstations in your classroom will be housed and used by students. Decisions about the kinds of containers used to store workstation tasks and about what is housed in these containers impact the success and efficiency of Math Workshop. Be sure the materials for tasks may reasonably be accommodated in storage containers. Having the needed materials at hand in the workstation container means that there is less student movement within the classroom during Math Workshop. While some student traffic may be necessary to retrieve needed items, remember that students who remain in their assigned workspaces are more likely to be on task. The more movement, the more distraction—not only for students who are moving, but also for students working at other workstations. When students must leave workspaces to get materials, limit the disruption by explaining to them how to go directly to the materials and back without interacting with other students. Include a list of the materials so that, as students clean their workspaces, they can be sure all the materials for the task have been returned.

With the GUIDE workshop model, each workstation contains multiple math tasks for students. Teachers must first decide where workstation tasks will be stored. The choice of workstation containers should depend on a number of variables.

➡ **Where will you store workstation containers in your classroom?** In classrooms with little space, containers should be stackable. Containers might be lined up along a wall or under an interactive whiteboard to make use of available space. Containers may also be placed on a table or counter top. In some classrooms, there may be space for a rolling set of drawers to neatly store workstation materials. Whatever containers you decide to use, be sure they can be comfortably accommodated in your classroom.

➡ **What kinds of tasks will be housed in the workstation containers?** Some teachers choose to store only essential workstation items in the containers. Students then assume responsibility of getting any other materials they need for the task. Other teachers choose to include all items that students will need, thus minimizing student movement in the classroom. So, consider what you plan to store in your workstation containers to determine size.

➡ **What kinds of containers do you have or can you afford to purchase?** In practical terms, teachers often have to make do with containers they have. So, instead of matching containers to the classroom space, sometimes teachers simply have to find the space to accommodate what they have.

Once you have thought about these questions, choose the containers you will use. Here are some options:

➡ plastic stackable boxes with lids (preferably clear so contents can be identified easily)

➡ baskets (natural materials, plastic, or metal)

➡ plastic totes or bins

➡ sets of drawers on wheels

➡ plastic cubes

➡ metal pails

➡ three-ring binders with page protectors containing task directions and pockets for small materials

➡ extra-large resealable plastic bags

➡ cardboard boxes

Undoubtedly, the most commonly used containers are plastic storage boxes with lids that can be neatly stacked with labels clearly visible. These are especially useful in classrooms with limited space. Many workstations may be stored compactly using these containers. Furthermore, they are generally quite durable, are relatively inexpensive, and can readily accommodate all but the largest materials needed by students as they work.

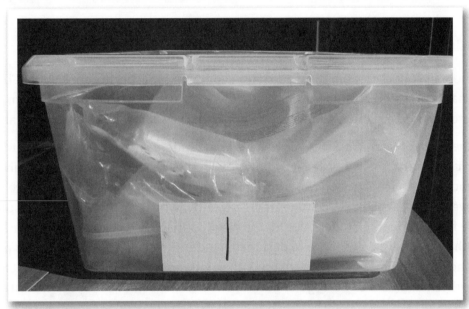

plastic storage box with Math Workstation label

The most inexpensive containers are cardboard boxes. Find a set of five matching boxes, with lids if possible, that are sturdy and an appropriate size. The exterior of the boxes may be painted or decorated however you like. Cover the edges of the boxes with packaging tape to reinforce their strength.

Once you have decided what kind of containers to use, label them clearly. With the GUIDE model, each container will be labeled with one letter of the GUIDE acronym. The sample workstation labels shown in Figure 2.3 can be found in the Digital Resources.

Figure 2.3 Sample GUIDE Workstation Labels

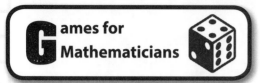

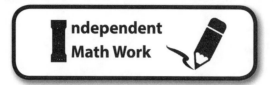

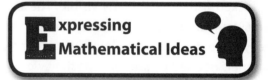

Workspace Locations

Decide where in your classroom the workstation containers will be stored. It should be an area that can be easily accessed by students as Math Workshop begins. Label the classroom area to indicate to students where these containers belong using the same labels as the container labels.

To make the most of Math Workshop time, have your students be responsible for retrieving workstation containers. Show them exactly how you would like this to be done, and give them plenty of practice with feedback on how they are doing. Develop a method to indicate which students have this duty each day so students clearly know who is responsible. The responsibility might rotate from student to student during the week so that all students have this task at one time or another. Teachers may choose to designate students responsible for materials on their Math Workshop management board, perhaps with color-coding. For instance, students whose names are written in blue are in charge of getting any materials needed for the workstation that day.

To minimize time spent setting up workstations, clearly designate workspace areas in your classroom for workstations rather than having students choose where they should go. This also allows you to place quieter workstations closer to the small-group lesson area and to strategically place other workstations close to materials that may be needed for those tasks.

Teach your students how the workspaces should be cleaned at the end of Math Workshop, returning all workstation materials neatly to their containers. Students in charge of retrieving workstation containers should then return them to the storage areas. Give students specific instruction regarding your expectations. Once they know what your expectations are, provide them with opportunities to practice.

The GUIDE workstation labels shown in Figure 2.3 may also be used to identify workspace locations in the classroom. Figure 2.4 shows a strategic classroom layout of GUIDE workstation locations that is described below.

➡ *Games for Mathematicians* is located in the math corner where a variety of games are stored. Students may spread out to work on the floor in this workstation. The noise level may be a bit higher with this workstation, so it is located well away from the small-group lesson.

➡ *Using What We Know* is located in the large-group area of the classroom where students may gather materials they may need for problem-solving tasks. Shelves in this area may be used to store manipulatives, copies of class-made anchor charts for student reference, and other resources students may need as they use what they know to solve problems.

➡ *Independent Math Work* is placed at tables or desks where students may work independently to review and reinforce their understanding of previously mastered concepts and skills. This is a relatively quiet workstation, so students may work in closer proximity to the small-group lesson.

➡ *Developing Fluency* is situated by the interactive whiteboard and sets of desks. Students may play games or complete tasks to improve their computational fluency at the interactive whiteboard or work at the desks.

➡ *Expressing Mathematical Ideas* is located at the computers. The use of technology encourages students to express their mathematical thinking in a variety of ways. From using simple word processing programs for math journal tasks to completing research projects, to creating digital slideshow presentations, to illustrating math problems, technology may enhance mathematical communication skills of students. With the proliferation of digital devices in school, many of these activities may occur anywhere in the classroom. Note that none of these technology options are required for this workstation. Any tasks that promote the learning of mathematical vocabulary and mathematical communication may be accomplished with recording sheets or in math journals.

Figure 2.4 Sample GUIDE Workstation Locations

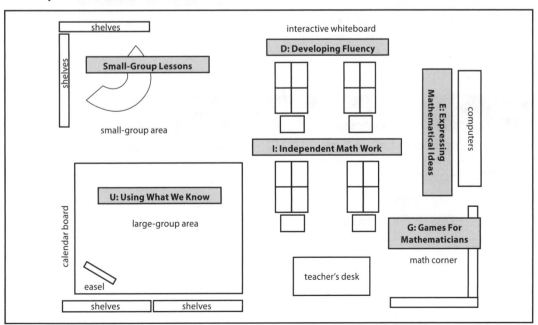

Math Workstation Contents

Because students do not rotate from station to station with the GUIDE model, each workstation contains numerous differentiated tasks—some mandatory, others optional. To minimize student confusion, tasks must be presented and described in student-friendly ways. Students need to know the tasks that are available at each station, whether they are mandatory or optional, and the task directions. When tasks include differentiation options, students must be able to identify which options they should complete and the directions for completing them.

For teachers who are using a workshop model other than GUIDE, adapt these strategies to fit the model you are using.

Workstation Task Menu

The Task Menu lists the tasks that are included in the workstation. It should clearly indicate which of them students must do and which of them are optional. Tasks with differentiation options should also be designated.

To make the menu accessible for all students, consider including a digital device in each workstation. To help students who have difficulty reading, you may record the menu so that they can listen to it orally. Using a digital device, you may also provide task directions or links to other resources and podcasts that will support student learning. A sample Workstation Task Menu is shown in Figure 2.5.

Figure 2.5 Sample GUIDE Workstation Task Menu (Grades 3–5)

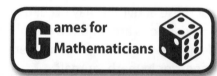

GUIDE Task Menu

Must Do	
Math Workstation task	**"Just right" task**
• Area and Perimeter War • 3-D Dimensional Figure Memory	✓
May Do	
Math Workstation task	**"Just right" task**
• Difference from 5,000	✓
• Vocabulary Bingo	
• Place Value I Have/Who Has	✓

If you store your workstations in a plastic storage box with a lid, the menu may be taped inside the lid to prevent it from being misplaced or damaged. For other storage containers, consider placing the menu in a page protector sleeve to prevent it from being damaged as students work.

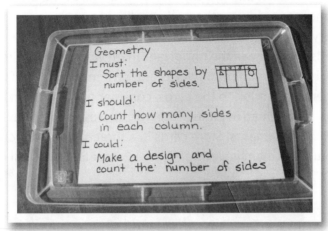

Task Menu inside workstation container lid

Math Workstation Tasks

Before including a math task in a workstation, always introduce it first in either a small-group or whole-class lesson. Students are expected to work independently during Math Workshop, so think carefully about what they will need to be successful as you prepare for these tasks. Effective Math Workstation tasks include explicit directions in student-friendly language. Student Task cards should clarify any confusion students may have as they perform the tasks. No matter how well you believe you have explained tasks or how well you think your students understood them, there will be times when students will need more directions. When no directions are provided and students are confused, they will either interrupt the small-group lesson being taught or become frustrated and unengaged. Figure 2.6 shows a sample of a Student Task card. The workstation task can be found on pages 102–104 and in the Digital Resources.

Figure 2.6 Sample Student Task Card (Grades 3–5)

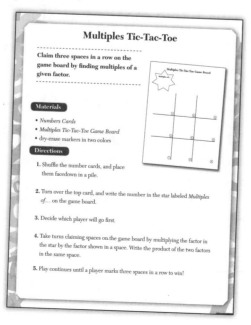

One of the benefits of having students work in pairs or small groups is the opportunity for them to talk about their mathematical thinking with their peers. One of the drawbacks, however, is that the teacher is not there to model mathematical talk or to encourage the use of appropriate mathematical vocabulary. One way to address these drawbacks is to create Talking Points cards for each task. These cards should have the important math words that are relevant to the task and may also have visual representations of words and sentence stems to facilitate mathematical discourse. To draw students' attention to the cards, consider printing them on brightly colored paper. Laminate them or insert them in page protector sleeves so they may be reused in the future for either the same task or similar tasks. Store cards in a three-ring binder organized by domains for easy access when you need them again. See Figure 2.7 for a sample Talking Points card.

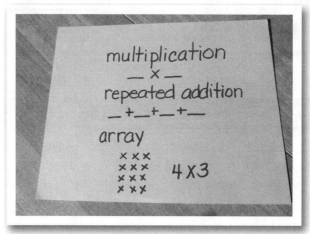

visual representations of math vocabulary words

Figure 2.7 Sample Talking Points Card (Grades K–2)

Talking Points

Vocabulary	Talk like a mathematician:
• add • addend • addition • double • plus • sum	I marked the sum _____ because _____ plus _____ equals _____. _____ is the sum of _____ and _____. The addends I chose are _____ and _____ because they have a sum of _____. The strategy I used to choose my addends is _____.

Workstation Management Boards

A well-planned workstation management board makes Math Workshop flow smoothly. By consulting the board, students know exactly where they will work during Math Workshop, thus eliminating the need for the teacher to give assignments orally during limited workshop time. Chapter 1 (pages 21–33) shows examples of workstation management boards for various workshop models. Use those as guides when you create a management board system for your Math Workshop.

Some teachers choose to create their own boards, some purchase commercially available management boards, and some use interactive whiteboard technology to display workshop assignments for students. Whatever type of workstation management board you choose, be sure that it

➡ clearly shows students where they should be working at any given time;

➡ is consistent; and

➡ is easy to change—either in workstations or in group composition.

Principles for a Workshop Learning Community

Perhaps even more important than preparing the classroom and workstation materials is the task of preparing students for Math Workshop. Teach learners the value of strong work habits and instill in them a sense of being an important member of a learning community. Rely on these principles adapted from Guided Reading to establish a feeling of community among your students during Math Workshop (Fountas and Pinnell 2001). All members of a Math Workshop community will

➡ assume responsibility for their own learning and for helping others learn;

➡ efficiently use their time to complete assigned math tasks;

➡ monitor their behavior to maximize their own learning and that of their fellow students; and

➡ keep workspaces and materials in order to support a productive Math Workshop for all members of the community.

Review and Reflect

1. Reflect on your current classroom arrangement. How can you make the arrangement more conducive to Math Workshop?

2. Take an informal inventory of the math resources in your classroom. Which of those do you use most often? Are there any that are rarely used? If so, is it because they are not needed or because they are difficult to access? How can you improve the storage of these resources?

3. Assembling Math Workstation tasks can be time consuming. In what ways can you work collaboratively with other teachers to create a collection of tasks for Math Workshop?

Managing Math Workshop

While many teachers are enthusiastic about the Guided Math framework, the idea of managing Math Workshop may be daunting. Traditional instruction has mainly been teacher centered. Students have been asked to assume very little responsibility for their own learning. Instead of thinking independently, young mathematicians have been encouraged to faithfully follow the directions of their teachers. With this instructional model, students have had few opportunities to learn how to work effectively with others, to solve problems that may occur when working with peers, to draw on their mathematical knowledge to solve problems, or to monitor their own learning. Because this type of instruction is what most teachers experienced as students, it often provides a sense of security for them. For better or worse, many teachers cling to the sense of control inherent to traditional instruction.

Teachers are rightly concerned about the efficacy of Math Workshop management practices because of their potential instructional impact. Effective management practices springboard student learning and allow teachers to extend their mathematics instruction in a myriad of ways—informal assessment of mathematics proficiency through observation and conversation as students work, the encouragement of deeper student thinking through well-crafted questions, one-on-one conferences with students, and differentiated small-group lessons. Poor workshop management, however, too often results in a chaotic classroom environment where little learning takes place.

Chaos can be avoided, though. The first steps in managing an effective Math Workshop are developing routines and procedures that define and clarify your expectations for students as they work independently and devising a system to hold students accountable for their independent work.

Developing Effective Routines and Procedures for Students

In creating routines and procedures for your classroom, take time to envision how you would like to see Math Workshop function with your students. As you picture your students working independently, think about how you would like them to behave. What responsibilities do you want them to assume? Imagine not only the broad overview of student behavior, but also consider the everyday problems that students may encounter as they work. How would you like students to handle these problems? Unless you have gone through the process of envisioning your expectations for students, there is little chance they will be able to meet your expectations.

Establish routines and procedures that address the most common problems students encounter in Math Workshop. Give them guidance on how to respond to issues that may arise to prevent the interruption of small-group lessons or student disengagement from workshop tasks. It is important, however, that the number of workshop norms you establish be reasonable. Too many overly detailed norms overwhelm students and are difficult to refer to as students work. To limit the number of behavioral norms, condense your expectations for students into overarching guidelines that will govern their behavior in the variety of situations they may encounter in Math Workshop.

For new teachers who have had little experience in the classroom, envisioning how Math Workshop will operate and anticipating specific student needs is challenging. Even veteran teachers may be so accustomed to their own management systems that they find it hard to envision alternative strategies. If you are in the process of developing routines and procedures for Math Workshop, collaborate with your peers. What kinds of routines and procedures have they established? What have they found successful? What problems have they experienced? The more you know about the various routines and procedures used by other teachers, the more options you have to choose from as you establish your own.

In addition to consulting with others, visit classrooms of teachers who have well-managed Math Workshops to find out how they manage their workshop time. Very effective teachers may have trouble describing what they do to support an effective Math Workshop because it comes naturally to them. If possible, obtain release time to visit and observe these classrooms at the beginning of the school year to learn how teachers establish effective Math Workshop learning environments.

When developing the routines and procedures for Math Workshop, take into consideration the questions below. Remember—there is no one *right* set of routines and procedures. Those that you establish should reflect the workshop model you are using, your preferences as a teacher, your classroom arrangement, and the needs of your students.

As Math Workshop Begins

➡ How will students get Math Workstations from where they are stored? Who will be responsible for this task? What are your expectations for behavior as students retrieve workstations? Do you expect them to walk—not run—to where workstations are stored and to take the most direct routes? Do you mind if they talk to other students as they carry out this task?

➡ How would you like other group members to move to the location of their Math Workstation? Are certain movement patterns in your classroom better than others? How do you expect students to behave as they move?

➡ If additional materials are needed to begin workstation tasks, how will students get them?

➡ If students do not understand tasks as Math Workshop begins, what should they do? Do you want to take time at the beginning of Math Workshop to be certain everyone understands the tasks?

➡ What voice levels should students use as they work? How will you let students know if they are getting too loud? What are the consequences if the noise level remains too high?

➡ Are students expected to remain in their workspaces until it is time to transition? Or, may students move from their workspaces for specific reasons (e.g., to gather additional materials, to confer with other groups, to use the restroom)? If so, what are acceptable reasons for movement?

➡ What do students do if needed materials are not available? Will you routinely provide alternative tasks in case there is a problem with one of the assigned tasks so you will not be interrupted?

➡ What should students do if technology is not working properly? Will you have a designated student technology expert they can consult? Or, should they work on an alternative task?

➡ What would you like students to do if they have questions about tasks after work has begun? Will you have a way they may indicate that they do not understand without interrupting you? For example, some classrooms have red and green cups for each station. If the cups are stacked so the green on is on top, everything is going smoothly. But, if cups are stacked so the red cup is on top, it sends the message that the group has questions and needs help. In this way, teachers are not interrupted, but get the message when groups need assistance.

➡ What should students do if they complete all workstation tasks? Will you provide alternative tasks?

➡ How should students deal with disruptive or uncooperative peers?

➡ How do you want students to deal with a true emergency (e.g., someone is sick or injured, there is a student with a major behavioral problem)?

➡ If you are using a rotational model for Math Workshop, how will you signal students that it is time to clean up and rotate to another workstation? Will you give an early warning so they have time to conclude their work and clean up their workspaces?

As Math Workshop Ends

➡ Will you give a warning signal prior to the end of Math Workshop so students can complete their work and clean up before the end of the workshop period? How will you signal the end of the workshop period? What responsibilities do student have as the workshop ends?

➡ Who is responsible for putting Math Workstations away? What are the procedures for putting materials away?

➡ If work is to be turned in, where should it be placed?

➡ When and how should students return to their desks or individual workspaces?

Holding Students Accountable During Math Workshop

Because students work independently during Math Workshop, it is important to have an efficient way to hold them accountable for quality work. Paper-and-pencil work may be turned in to document what was accomplished with workstation tasks. Many of the Math Workstation tasks provided in this book include task-specific recording sheets or graphic organizers. But, when that is not the case, how can you generate a sense of accountability in students working independently during Math Workshop?

You may choose to circulate among your students to monitor their independent work. This might mean focusing on their ability to work independently or on their mathematical capabilities. If you choose to monitor in this way, allow ample time to converse with students rather than immediately correcting their errors. Given time, students will often discover their own errors and move to correct them. They learn much more from this experience than from teachers coming to the rescue. When teachers step in too soon to point out errors, students are deprived of the opportunity to identify and correct their mistakes on their own. Consider the following strategies to motivate students to be responsible independent learners:

➡ **Help your students view themselves as mathematicians and recognize their responsibility to learn the craft of mathematicians during Math Workshop.** Emphasize the fact those "who do the work do the learning" (Hoffer 2012, 52). By creating a learning community culture, you set the stage for serious academic pursuit by students. Talk with your class every day about the purposes of Math Workshop activities that students will complete. Encourage students to discuss their ideas of what characterizes a mathematics learning community. Have them share what they see as their responsibilities in creating this kind of community. Nurturing a sense of responsibility for their own learning not only encourages accountability as students work, but also helps them develop soft skills, such as curiosity, persistence, making use of their abilities, and being skillful collaborators—all of which are essential for lifelong learning. These thinking or learning dispositions (Claxton, Costa, and Kallick 2016) are fundamental to student success in the twenty-first century.

➡ **Encourage students to self-assess their own work efforts as they participate in Math Workshop.** It has long been recognized that self-assessment is an integral part of effective education (McTighe and O'Connor 2005; Davies 2000; Black and Wiliam 1998). During Math Workshop, this kind of reflection strengthens students' perceptions of themselves as mathematicians and active learners. Self-assessment may focus either on academic progress, on work behavior, or both.

Prompt students to reflect on their mathematical understanding and on the quality of their work by having them respond to questions such as:

➡ What parts of your work show evidence that you have met the criteria for quality work?

➡ What part(s) of your work can be improved? What will you do to improve it?

➡ How do you rate your understanding? Why?

➡ What can you do to extend your learning?

➡ What are your next steps in learning?

(Sammons 2013)

To facilitate the self-monitoring of their work behavior, have students complete one of the following activities:

➡ **Think and Evaluate**—During the last few minutes of Math Workshop, ask students to think about how well they assumed responsibility for their own learning. In a math journal or on a recording sheet, have students rate how well they did on a scale of one star to five stars— where five stars means "all-star" work, three stars means they did "just okay" work, and one star means they did a poor job. In addition, it is important that students explain why they evaluated themselves as they did. This activity may be used either to self-assess individual work or for students to rate group work. The Think and Evaluate Self-Assessment shown in Figure 3.1 can be found in the Digital Resources for each grade-level band: K–2, 3–5, and 6–8.

Figure 3.1 Sample Think and Evaluate Self-Assessment (Grades 3–5)

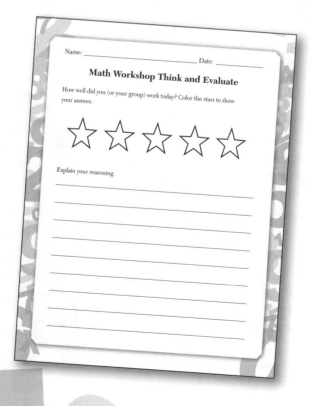

➡ **Math Workshop Expectations Checklist**—Give students a checklist (see Figure 3.2) with some or all of the routines and procedures that have been established for Math Workshop. Ask students to rate themselves on how well they did with each workshop behavior. At the end of the checklist, have them describe what they plan to do to improve their workshop learning experience. The Expectations Checklist Self-Assessment shown in Figure 3.2 can be found in the Digital Resources for each grade-level band: K–2, 3–5, and 6–8.

Figure 3.2 Sample Expectations Checklist Self-Assessment (Grades 3–5)

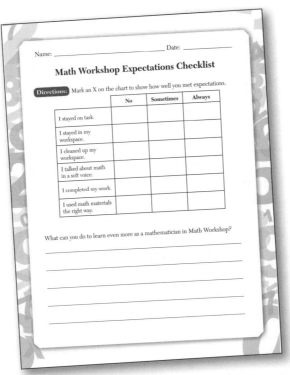

➡ **Recording Work**—Have students record their work in math journals, on recording sheets, or through the use of digital devices. This is one of the most efficient ways of holding students accountable for their work during Math Workshop. While some work may be paper-and-pencil tasks, other tasks that may be recorded are the individual student's work or outcome for each round in a math game. With the widespread use of technology in classrooms, additional recording options are often available. Apps on digital devices provide students with the means to record auditory explanations of their work, to take photographs of their mathematical efforts, or to generate digital representations of their thinking.

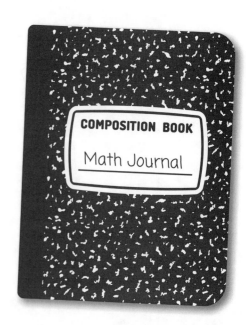

For instance, if students are playing the Multiplication War game in which students draw two cards, compute the product, and then decide who has the greater product, the recording sheet might look like the sample shown in Figure 3.3.

Figure 3.3 Sample Recording Sheet

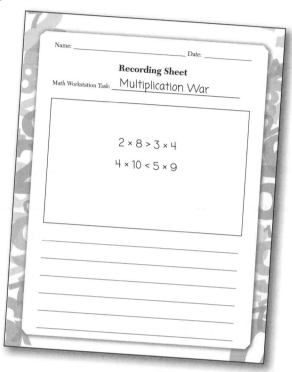

To quickly check student work, have students display their journals or their recording sheets on their desks. This may be done when they return from their workstations at the end of Math Workshop. Circulate to briefly check student work. If it is inconvenient to do this at the end of Math Workshop, ask students to turn in their recording sheets or math journals open to the work of the day. Check their work at the end of the school day. Look for two things: that the work was completed accurately and that there was a sufficient amount of work completed. A check mark or stamp will show students that you have checked their work. This student work does not need to be graded or sent home to parents. If technology is being used to record student work, you may be able to digitally access the data. Students may be able to send their work digitally for review.

Immediately identify the causes of any problems you notice and address accountability issues with students as they arise. When you discover problems with students' independent work, first search to determine the root causes. Once you identify the causes, you are well on your way to finding solutions to the problems. Follow these strategies for targeting problems and strengthening students' work habits during Math Workshop.

➡ **Mistakes**—Should you discover too many mistakes in a student's work, confer with the student one-on-one to learn whether the errors resulted from mathematical misconceptions or from carelessness on the part of the student. Often, students are able to identify their mistakes as they share their mathematical thinking in one-on-one conferences—*if* they understand the math. When careless mistakes occur, it may indicate that the problem is due to haste or lack of effort. On the other hand, if a student's mathematical understanding is the issue, these conferences provide valuable insight into the kinds of misconceptions students may have—misconceptions that may be addressed either in the conference or in subsequent small-group lessons.

➡ **Misconceptions**—If mathematical misconceptions are affecting the quality of students' independent work, provide additional instruction targeted to specific needs to increase understanding and skill. This is *not* a time for a general reteaching. To maximize the effectiveness of your instruction, find out exactly what it is that students do not know or understand and focus on that as you reteach. You may choose to do this as a teaching point during a conference with an individual student or, if several students share the same misconception, during a targeted small-group lesson.

➡ **Attention**—If errors appear to be due to carelessness, share your concerns with students. One way to encourage greater attention to work is to give students the opportunity to work beside you during Math Workshop the following day. This will make it easier for students to concentrate. Because students enjoy working independently, they are usually highly motivated to avoid this "opportunity" in the future.

➡ **Completion of Work**—If one or two students are not completing a sufficient amount of work during Math Workshop, tackle the problem at once. This problem can be contagious if left unchecked. Talk with students to find out why work is incomplete. These students may also be given the "opportunity" to work beside you the next day. With close proximity, you may supervise their independent work and encourage them to put more effort into it. This strategy will also motivate them to improve their work habits so they may once again work independently.

➡ **Engagement**—If too many students are unengaged during Math Workshop, it is important to stop and reflect on the effectiveness of your workshop management. Ask yourself: Have you created a learning culture in your classroom where students are expected to assume individual responsibility as mathematicians? If not, refocus your efforts on promoting this kind of culture. Do the routines and procedures you established for Math Workshop clearly define your expectations for students? If not, consider how you can revise them. Do students know the routines and procedures? If not, reteach them. Have students had ample opportunity to practice workshop routines and procedures? If not, provide more practice with timely and specific feedback for students. Suggested strategies for launching an effective Math Workshop are provided in Chapter 4 (pages 61–70).

Working with Mathematics Coaches

Many schools and districts now employ mathematics and/or academic coaches who help teachers enhance their mathematics instruction. Just as the best athletes rely on coaches, so should all teachers. Even the best can get better! Coaches can offer valuable advice as you implement Math Workshop. If you plan collaboratively with colleagues, invite your coach to join your meetings. Share your plans with your coaches so they may offer their feedback based on their prior experience. In addition, take advantage of some of the other opportunities coaches can provide to support implementation of Math Workshop, such as the following:

➡ **Peer visits**—Coaches can often arrange for teachers to visit other classrooms during Math Workshop. These peer visits allow you to observe Math Workshop, uninterrupted, as students work and teachers teach. If you are fortunate enough to visit other classrooms to observe Math Workshop, take notes to document what you notice, and jot down any questions you have for the teacher. Teachers learn the most from these experiences when they meet with the teacher and coach subsequent to the observation. Teachers may reflect on what they saw and ask any questions they may have concerning the room set-up or the routines and procedures followed by students. The ideas you garner during peer observations may be used and adapted to refine your own Math Workshop.

➡ **Co-teach opportunities**—Coaches are sometimes willing to co-teach in a classroom to support the implementation of new instructional strategies. If you are hesitant to take the first leap into Math Workshop, a coach may help ease you in by being in the classroom for the first few workshop sessions. When you are teaching a small-group lesson, it may be difficult to assess the functionality of the routines and procedures. If a coach teaches a small-group lesson, you can observe students working independently to assess the effectiveness of the routines and procedures you have created and taught. Or, as you teach a lesson, a coach monitoring students as they work independently may remind them of behavioral and academic expectations you have established and also give you constructive feedback.

➡ **Observations**—Even after implementing Math Workshop, experienced teachers may turn to coaches to help them address problems that arise. Sometimes having another set of eyes in the classroom during Math Workshop offers a whole new perspective. Coaches understand problems that may surface when students work independently. In classrooms acting solely as observers, coaches can focus on the issues that are troubling you to get to the heart of the problem. By working together—teacher and coach—workshop problems can be resolved.

➡ **Resources**—Coaches can provide a wealth of information. They can also assist teachers in obtaining resources needed for Math Workshop. To stay current on curriculum and instruction, maintain a close relationship with your coach, as most coaches keep up-to-date in these areas. Moreover, coaches can often locate and provide materials you may need for Math Workshop. Share your resource needs with your coach. Coaches can sometimes locate the supplies you lack in your building or district. In addition, they may be able to use their funding, or school or district funding, to purchase materials you need.

Joining Professional Learning Communities

If you do not have a math coach in your school or district, you may continue to learn and grow by joining a Professional Learning Community (PLC). Teachers grow by reading, planning, reflecting, and working together. Become an effective teacher leader by taking an active role. Share your knowledge and expertise, continue to educate yourself, and examine your teaching practices with your colleagues. Sammons (2015) provides a detailed yearlong PLC plan for the implementation of Guided Math—one month of which focuses exclusively on the implementation of Math Workshop (see Appendix B).

If the implementation of Math Workshop is a new experience for you, it may be reassuring to work with colleagues when you try out new ideas. PLC members collaborate in developing plans to meet their own specific learning interests and needs. A PLC may be a perfect incubator for the implementation of Math Workshop.

Review and Reflect

1. Reflect on how you envision student behaviors during Math Workshop. Jot down notes describing how students will behave as Math Workshop begins, as they work during Math Workshop, and as Math Workshop ends. What should students know and be able to do to make this vision a reality?

2. What are your greatest concerns about holding students accountable as they work independently during Math Workshop? What measures can you take to ensure that students are fully engaged and doing their best work?

3. If you are in the process of implementing Math Workshop or are seeking to improve the Math Workshop structure you are now using, what support can you draw upon in your school or school district?

Planning Math Workstations

While you should select and implement a Math Workshop model that is most compatible with your mode of teaching and the needs of your students, this chapter focuses on the GUIDE model because of its ease of implementation and the instructional flexibility it offers teachers. The information in this chapter, however, may be adapted to any workshop model, as may each of the GUIDE workstation tasks.

Strategies for Implementing GUIDE Math Workstations

GUIDE workstations are most successful when teachers give careful attention to the composition of their student groups, the mathematics content of the workstation tasks, and the types of math tasks students are expected to complete. Follow these guidelines to establish a productive GUIDE workshop in your classroom.

Grouping Students with the GUIDE Model

It is important to understand that with the GUIDE model for Math Workshop, students *do not* rotate from workstation to workstation. Instead, students work in only one station per day and will have rotated to all five of the GUIDE stations by the end of a week. Therefore, the composition of the workstation groups is different from the groups for small-group lessons.

Different groups of learners work at the five GUIDE workstations during Math Workshop. Students work on multiple tasks at one station for the entire Math Workshop period unless called to a small-group lesson or conference. Instead of groups rotating to a teacher lesson, teachers call students with similar learning needs for targeted and differentiated small-group lessons. Meanwhile, other students continue working on workstation tasks. When a small-group lesson or conference is completed, those students return to their workstations. For that reason, the composition of groups working in GUIDE workstations may be heterogeneous. This means that students of varying levels of mathematical knowledge and skill have chances to work together during Math Workshop.

Although students may be permitted to choose Math Workstations and where they will work each day, teacher-assigned workstation groups are generally most effective. Rely on your knowledge of students to create five well-balanced groups and assign them to workstations each day. That way, you ensure that groups include students of various learning levels who will work together well, and students who have difficulty getting along are separated. Selecting group compositions also offers you great flexibility in developing students' social and work skills. Students may be encouraged to broaden their horizons by working with peers they may not normally work with, assume leadership roles within these heterogeneous workshop groups, or improve their work habits by learning from other group members. Strategically use what you know about your students to help them benefit from these cooperative work experiences. Figure 4.1 provides guidelines to keep in mind when creating GUIDE workstation groups.

Figure 4.1 Guidelines for Creating GUIDE Workstation Groups

What to Do	What Not to Do
• Use what you know about your students, including work habits and learning needs, to create balanced groups. • Include students with a variety of learning needs in each group. • Try to ensure that each group has students who are capable of acting as problem solvers for the group. • Create groups of equal size. • Try to have an even number of students in each group, whenever possible, so students may work in pairs. • Change the composition of groups every month.	• Group students together who have difficulty getting along. • Include best friends in the same group consistently. • Compose groups that consist of talkative students or very quiet students. • Place too many extremely active students in the same group. • Hesitate to change the composition of a group when it is not working well. • Consistently change groups each week. • Maintain the same groupings for more than a month. • Create homogeneous *high, middle,* and *low* groups.

Effective Tasks for Math Workstations

66 *The learning opportunities that teachers create are the prime vehicles for propelling learning in classrooms. Without the right vehicles, learning slows down, loses momentum, and in some cases comes to a standstill, producing parking lots rather than speedways* 99

(Ritchart 2015, 144).

Some of the most important decisions you make when planning for Math Workshop are those regarding the kinds of tasks to incorporate in GUIDE workstations. These learning vehicles can either propel student learning or slow it to a halt. Math Workshop functions most effectively when workstation tasks are "Goldilocks" tasks—not too easy, not too hard. These "just right" tasks offer worthwhile learning experiences that students may complete independently and accurately.

If tasks are not challenging enough, they waste the time of students who could, instead, be engaged in work that helps them grow as mathematicians. Students become bored and, as a result, discipline problems often arise. On the other hand, tasks that are too difficult present even greater problems. If students are not sure of what they need to do or how to go about completing an assigned task, it is understandable that their first impulse is to ask for help. Yet, during Math Workshop, when teachers are teaching small-group lessons or conducting conferences, students are taught not to interrupt. Frustrated, students may interrupt the teacher anyway, complete the assigned task incorrectly, or become disengaged. None of these options are desirable.

The types of tasks listed below are prime vehicles for Math Workstations that propel rather than slow the momentum of student learning during Math Workshop.

➡ **Tasks that support practice, review, or maintenance of previously mastered concepts or skills**—Students should be able to carry out tasks they are assigned independently and accurately. Refrain from immediately assigning practice of content currently being taught (Sammons 2013). If students were already capable of doing that work accurately and independently, you would not be teaching it. Instead, Math Workstation tasks should have content that is already understood by students.

Returning periodically to apply and practice previously learned material is often referred to as *distributed practice*. Research shows that this kind of practice increases the likelihood that mathematical understanding and skill will become part of students' permanent memory, and thus retained (Marzano 2007). In addition to immediate learning benefits, less review time is needed when students continue to engage in distributed practice regularly over the course of an academic year. As a result, more time may be devoted to teaching and learning of new mathematical content.

➡ **Tasks that require students to complete work from a previous lesson**—Because there may be limited time during small-group lessons, there should be a greater emphasis on quality over quantity when choosing problems for lessons. When teachers selectively assign only the problems that are most effective at promoting understanding and competence, they use only a fraction of the problems provided in math textbook lessons. The remaining problems may be incorporated into workstation tasks in the coming days or weeks as distributed practice.

➡ **Tasks that promote computational fluency**—Computational fluency is a key component of mathematical literacy. Accordingly, most math standards require that students obtain automaticity when performing basic operations with one-digit numbers. Research indicates that learners gain automaticity by developing number sense—by honing their "ability to work flexibly with numbers, decomposing them and regrouping them with confidence" (Boaler 2014, 471). This process takes time, however, and Boaler warns, "it cannot be accelerated by methods that encourage speed at the expense of understanding" (473).

Math Workshop presents an ideal time for students to engage in activities that develop number sense and computational fluency. Rather than relying on timed tests to teach math facts, provide other opportunities for students to become computationally fluent. Provide games and number activities that teach number sense and mental math strategies in Math Workstations. For older students, provide problems that require them to apply strategies for efficient computation. Students may successfully complete these worthwhile tasks by working independently. Regularly including these types of Math Workstation tasks allows students ample time to develop number sense without the intense added pressure of speed that causes so many students anxiety. Older students have opportunities to apply computational strategies they have acquired to solve more complex problems.

➡ **Tasks that encourage mathematical exploration**—Free exploration to answer a thought-provoking question is often a catalyst for spurring inquisitive thinking. Tasks based on these types of questions also spur mathematical curiosity.

The complexity of tasks may vary dramatically. For example, students need opportunities to interact with unfamiliar manipulatives before they learn how to use them to extend mathematical understanding or solve problems. As students explore new manipulatives, they may explain what they notice about the manipulatives, how they are the same or different from other manipulatives they have used, or how they think they might be used to help them learn about math. Students may also take photographs using digital devices and list all of the math connections they observe in the pictures. Students might be challenged to use a variety of manipulatives to solve the same problem, document how each was used with a photo, determine which was most efficient, and then justify their thinking.

For more complex tasks, students may engage in a Science, Technology, Engineering, and Mathematics (STEM) activity. For example, students might decide how to build the strongest bridge using straws, pasta, toothpicks, or craft sticks. They learn to problem solve as they explore what makes one design stronger than another. Students might also be asked to collect a set of data to analyze and answer questions such as: *What do you notice about the data collected? Are there any patterns? What can you learn from the data?* Whenever possible, build upon the interests and curiosity of your students when creating these tasks.

➡ **Tasks that require the creation of a product to represent mathematical thinking**—While this type of task may overlap with several others, it is important to highlight it because of the thinking processes that students must go through to create a product representing something they have learned, a problem they have solved, or a discovery they have made. In deciding how to best make thinking visible (Ritchart 2015; Hattie 2009), students must thoroughly understand their own mathematical thinking and then decide how to communicate it clearly. As you plan Math Workstation tasks, consider how you can challenge your students to represent their thinking.

Whether students are asked to create posters illustrating their problem-solving processes, digital slideshows to explain what they have learned, or graphic displays of data that justify their conclusions, students must thoroughly examine their thinking. Although it is important to provide criteria, resist the temptation to provide a template for the product. Encourage students to visualize their mathematical reasoning and give them the freedom to be creative. Thinking processes students go through to complete these tasks are as important, if not more so, than the products they create. Help students understand the value of the entire thinking process so they are not tempted to take shortcuts as they create their products.

Compulsory or Optional Workstation Tasks

Students remain at the *same* GUIDE workstations throughout the Math Workshop block, but the amount of time students work at a station may vary from day to day. Those who spend little or no time in small-group lessons or teacher conferences will have much more time to engage in workstation tasks. Include ample and varied tasks at each workstation to keep these students productively engaged. Others may spend a significant amount of workshop time in lessons or conferences, which leaves them a minimal amount of time for workstation tasks. Too many compulsory tasks may be difficult for them to complete. Use your judgment as a teacher to create a balance between compulsory and optional tasks.

When planning tasks, include *both* compulsory tasks for all to complete and a selection of optional tasks for those students who have extra time. Students who have little time to work at stations because of lessons or conferences may not be able to complete the compulsory tasks. Make allowances for these learners. It is important to understand that small-group lessons and one-on-one conferences with you are far more valuable to students than the completion of independent work. They may also need your help in understanding this. Young learners should not be burdened by having to make up the workstation tasks that are missed because they are receiving additional instruction.

As you begin Math Workshop in your classroom, take time to observe students working independently to discover what you can realistically expect them to accomplish within a math period. Over time, you will get a feel for how long it takes them to complete tasks and how long games will keep their attention. Use your observations to help you decide how many compulsory tasks and how many optional tasks to include in each of the five GUIDE workstations.

Clearly indicate which workstation tasks have priority by labeling them on the Task Menu rather than simply *telling* students which must be completed. When students know exactly what they are required to do, they learn to tackle those tasks first and begin to develop valuable work habits.

Tips for Creating Math Workstation Tasks

Math Workstation tasks may be gathered from a variety of places. This resource provides a wide selection of workstation tasks for three grade-level bands (e.g., K–2, 3–5, 6–8), many of which may be adapted for other grade levels. After examining the tasks for the grade you teach, browse the tasks for the other grade-level bands for further ideas. Keep the following tips in mind when planning workstation tasks.

➡ **Plan tasks with specific academic goals in mind.** All tasks should align with mathematical content from grade-level standards. Avoid including tasks only because students will enjoy them or because they are convenient, unless they also reinforce concepts your students should be learning.

➡ **Provide tasks that make use of simple materials and have simple procedures.** With instructional time at a premium, tasks with familiar materials and simple procedures offer the advantage of requiring little introduction and preparation time. Consider including tasks that involve the use of number cards (playing cards), number cubes (dice), or dominos for all grade levels. Because these materials are readily available, the tasks are easy to prepare and minimize the math materials required.

➡ **Pull tasks from problems, games, and other materials that have been used to teach previous lessons.** Using existing resources makes planning easier, requires little introduction time, and provides ongoing distributive practice to help students develop deeper understanding and retain concepts and skills. Because small-group time is relatively short, teachers must use discretion in selecting the few problems that students will work on during the lesson. The remaining problems may be assigned as workstation tasks. Circling back to work on problems from previous lessons offers students ongoing distributive practice that deepens their mathematical understanding and improves retention.

➡ **Include tasks in which mathematical content may vary, but games or procedures remain the same.** The introduction of new games and tasks is time consuming and increases the probability that students will either do them incorrectly or become frustrated. There are many tasks, however, in which content may vary and be differentiated according to students' individual learning needs but basic procedures remain the same. An example is the classic card game War. Little time is needed to teach the game, yet the focus of the game may be changed according to the math concepts or skills to be reviewed. For primary learners, students may each draw a single card and compare the numbers to find which is greater. Older students might each draw two cards, create the greatest two-digit number possible, and then compare their numbers. Other variations might involve drawing two cards and then finding the sum or product of the numbers, creating the greatest possible fraction, or creating the greatest possible number with an exponent. Use your creativity to adapt games to content you want your students to practice and retain.

➡ **Change tasks purposefully.** Tasks do *not* have to be changed daily or even weekly. Because GUIDE workstations contain a number of related tasks, students may revisit them over several weeks. In contrast to math centers of the past that changed weekly, GUIDE workstation tasks are changed only for intentional instructional purposes.

➡ **Assemble a Math Workstations binder.** Eliminate the need to recreate materials for Math Workstations by assembling a binder of task materials. In the binder, store Task Menus and Talking Points cards along with lists of materials needed so you may easily find them for future use.

➡ **Plan collaboratively and share resources.** Collaborate with grade-level colleagues to share the preparation of Math Workstation tasks. Working collaboratively helps to streamline the workload and often results in greater creativity. Also consider vertical collaboration. Tasks from earlier grade levels may be included in workstations during the first few weeks of school. Students are already familiar with them, and they provide a good review of math content from the previous grade. These tasks may also be helpful prior to beginning a new unit and may minimize teacher-led class time reviewing prerequisite knowledge and skills for new content. As students master grade-level content and skills, tasks from the next grade level may offer additional challenge.

➡ **Create tasks from online education blogs, social media, and other sites**—The Internet has a multitude of sites dedicated to teaching ideas—some better than others. When researching instructional ideas, use your professional judgment and carefully evaluate resources before using them. It is important to assess the appropriateness of any materials you choose to include in Math Workstations. Before choosing a task because it "sounds fun" or maybe has engaging graphics, verify that it offers students a challenging experience that appropriately targets the standards for their grade level.

Incorporating Digital Devices into Math Workstations

Widespread availability of digital devices has transformed Math Workstations in many classrooms. The portability, flexibility, and ease-of-use of digital devices are popular with both teachers and students. Some schools now have Bring Your Own Device (BYOD) policies that increase the technological options available as well as address the challenges of effective use.

Instructional Uses for Digital Devices

A vast selection of mathematics programs and apps are available for classroom use. Their primary instructional uses are described below.

➡ **Providing math practice**—Digital devices in math classes are probably most frequently used for practice. Many apps are available in which students practice math skills as they play highly engaging games. Most of these are much like flashy worksheets and focus on fluency over comprehension. Some apps allow teachers to review student progress. While many of these objectives may be accomplished just as well with flash cards or worksheets, students are often more motivated and engaged when working in these apps.

➡ **Building mathematical comprehension**—Higher quality apps and digital resources focus more on math processes. They may employ visual models or video lessons to help students gain a greater understanding of math concepts. Some provide tutorials if students appear to need additional instruction. These are of greater value instructionally than those that focus exclusively on students' speedy answers.

➡ **Promoting engagement with mathematical practices and processes**—Technologies that are the most valuable encourage student creativity, critical thinking, and communication. Using these apps or programs, students devise ways to communicate their mathematical ideas orally, with representations, or in writing. Students might use word processing programs or digital slideshow presentations. Alternatively, they might opt to show their mathematical understanding by creating comics or animations with apps such as Comic Life©. Apps like Explain Everything™ allow students to illustrate and even record oral explanations of their thinking. With these kinds of apps, students move beyond simple rote learning (Pelton and Pelton 2012, Section 7) to more complex and challenging mathematical work.

➡ **Delivering instruction**—While technology will most likely never replace teachers, it can effectively deliver instruction. In addition to programs or apps that offer tutorial advice, students can also watch short video lessons. Companies such as Khan Academy have become sources of video lessons that may be readily accessed by students when they need further instruction.

➡ **Enabling flipped instruction**—Some teachers are implementing flipped instruction in their classrooms by taking advantage of prerecorded lessons found online, or recording the lessons themselves. Typically, with flipped instruction, students are asked to watch an instructional video for homework. The next day, the teacher addresses any questions students may have and then provides support as they practice what they learned from the video-recorded lesson. With Math Workshop, flipped instruction can assume another dimension. Students may watch the instructional video in a workstation in preparation for the next day's small-group lesson. Many of the problems of traditional flipped instruction (e.g., lack of technology at home, students who fail to watch the lesson) are avoided, yet the advantages of this instructional strategy remain. Moreover, incorporating these lessons into workstations uses technology in a way that encourages students to assume greater responsibility for their own learning.

Suggestions for Selecting Math Programs and Apps

Consider the suggestions listed below as you assess and select programs or apps for Math Workstations.

➡ Choose those that align with mathematics standards you are targeting.

➡ Look for those that offer students opportunities to review and maintain previously learned concepts and skills or build fluency in a variety of ways.

➡ Check for ease of understanding and use by students.

➡ Opt for those that focus on conceptual understanding and application before emphasizing fluency.

➡ Take into account support the program or app provides for students if they begin to struggle.

➡ Select those that differentiate to meet students' needs.

➡ Include programs or apps that allow you to track and review student progress.

➡ Assess the educational value of programs or apps on your own rather than relying too heavily on popularity or online ratings.

Management of Digital Devices

Using digital devices in Math Workshop generates much student enthusiasm. Although students may have had previous experiences using digital devices, it is important to give them opportunities to explore devices before they are added to workstations.

Once students have had hands-on time with digital devices, they will need clear guidance as to your expectations for their use during Math Workshop. Clearly establish and teach these procedures to students as you introduce Math Workshop.

Address the following questions as you develop procedures for the use of digital devices at Math Workstations.

➡ How will devices be distributed and collected?

➡ Who will work with devices and when?

➡ How will students know which programs or apps they should use?

➡ What are the expectations for student behavior when working with a device?

➡ What should students do if they do not understand a program or app? What should they do if the device does not function properly?

➡ How will students be held accountable for work on devices? If programs or apps do not provide a product or track progress, how will students document work?

➡ What are the consequences for improperly using devices (e.g., careless handling, not working on assigned tasks, not completing work)?

Differentiating Math Workstation Tasks

It is important that workstation tasks are differentiated to meet the unique needs of learners. Task Menus should clearly indicate which tasks have these options, and directions for these tasks should explain each of the options. Students need to know not only what the options are, but also which of them they should complete. Rather than labeling the options by achievement level, various options for differentiation may be indicated by color, shape, or other symbol. For example, if there are three options, one might be coded with a circle, one with a triangle, and one with a square. Let students know which options they will complete by assigning them to the shape that best meets their learning needs.

While much focus has been placed on differentiation for struggling students, differentiation for those who may need extra challenge is equally important. There are several ways to provide differentiation. Tasks may be differentiated by

➡ **providing completely different tasks**—In some instances, students at one workstation will work on completely different tasks to address identified needs of students.

➡ **providing variations of the same task**—This is the most efficient way to differentiate Math Workstation tasks because students work on the same task with some variations, so it can be introduced to everyone at the same time rather than having to introduce different tasks for different students. The task might be differentiated by changing the numbers, operations involved, or other aspects of the task to make it appropriate for all learners. Students who struggle with reading may require a recording of the task directions or other written materials. Some students may need to have manipulatives available. Others may benefit from having vocabulary cards with visual representations as references. Consider students' needs and offer support, if necessary, but use your professional judgment to avoid providing ongoing supports that become crutches rather than scaffolds for learning. Each task provided in this resource offers suggestions for differentiation to address individual students' needs.

➡ **providing multiple ways for students to show their learning**—Students who struggle may benefit from the use of manipulatives to demonstrate their mathematical understanding. Students who need a challenge may create graphic organizers to display their work or graphs to represent data.

Review and Reflect

1. What are the advantages of heterogeneous grouping of students? What are the advantages of homogeneous grouping? How can you provide students with opportunities to work in both kinds of groups during Math Workshop?

2. Consider the kinds of tasks recommended for workstations. How can you adapt resources that you currently use to create these tasks? Where else can you find ideas for Math Workstation tasks?

3. Digital devices can greatly impact student learning. In what ways can they be used to engage students in more than an entertaining drill of math skills?

Math Workstation Tasks

Without effective Math Workstation tasks, successfully implementing Math Workshop is impossible. Tasks must address appropriate student learning needs, offer options for differentiation, and provide needed support for independent work by students, without requiring enormous amounts of preparation by teachers. Often the best tasks are those derived from work done in small-group lessons that is assigned as ongoing distributive practice. Continued practice with these tasks helps students retain what they have learned and develop a deeper understanding of mathematical content. In addition, tasks that focus on improving students' computational fluency may be incorporated into Math Workstations effectively. Students may complete them independently without frustration, and they give students much needed practice to improve their automaticity.

The tasks in this chapter have been designed for use with the GUIDE Workshop Model, but they may be incorporated into any workshop model you choose. Sample workstation tasks per grade-level band (e.g., K–2, 3–5, 6–8) for each of the five GUIDE workstations are included. As you read these sample tasks, consider how their structure supports independent student work. Reflect on how you can modify resources you currently use to create math tasks for your classroom. Although these tasks are grouped by grade-level bands, many may be adapted for use by students in other grade levels. Use these samples to spur other ideas. Often the best Math Workstation tasks are those developed by teachers to meet the specific learning needs of their students, using materials that are simple and familiar to students.

An **overview** of the lesson, materials, objective, procedure, and differentiation is provided for the teacher on the first page of each GUIDE workstation task.

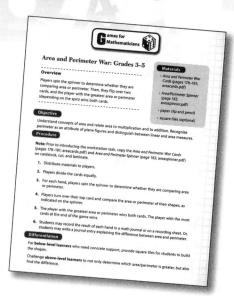

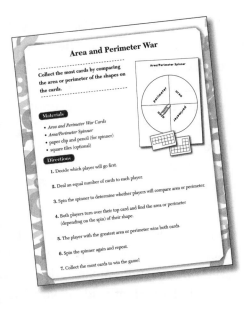

A **Student Task card** with directions and a materials list for the task is provided to help aid implementation and organization.

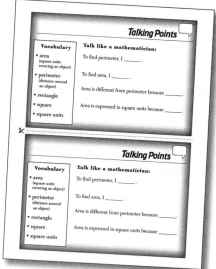

A **Talking Points card** with math vocabulary words and sentence stems is provided to encourage mathematical discourse.

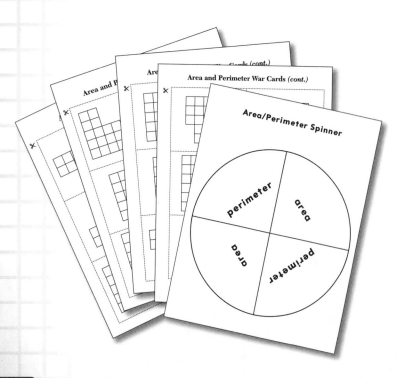

Additional **resources** for each task (e.g., spinners, cards, activity sheets) are included in Appendix C.

Figure 5.1 lists samples of GUIDE workstation tasks in this chapter. The tasks and additional resource materials may be found in the Digital Resources.

Figure 5.1 GUIDE Workstation Tasks

Workstation	Grade Band	Task
G	K–2	• *Race to the Bottom* (pages 72–74)
	3–5	• *Area and Perimeter War* (pages 75–77)
	6–8	• *Integer Tug-of-War* (pages 78–80)
U	K–2	• *Polygon Pictures* (pages 81–83)
	3–5	• *$1,000 House* (pages 84–86)
	6–8	• *Graphing Growing Patterns* (pages 87–89)
I	K–2	• *Piggy Bank Problems* (pages 90–92)
	3–5	• *Follow the Rule* (pages 93–95)
	6–8	• *Slope and Intercept* (pages 96–98)
D	K–2	• *Addition Move One* (pages 99–101)
	3–5	• *Multiples Tic-Tac-Toe* (pages 102–104)
	6–8	• *Scientific Notation* (pages 105–107)
E	K–2	• *Math Vocabulary Book* (pages 108–110)
	3–5	• *This Reminds Me Of…* (pages 111–113)
	6–8	• *Making Connections* (pages 114–116)

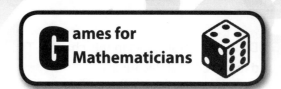

Games for **M**athematicians

Race to the Bottom: Grades K–2

Materials

- *120 Chart*
  (page 179; 120chart.pdf)

- paper clip and pencil

- game markers

- *Race to the Bottom Spinner* (page 180; spinner.pdf)

- base-ten blocks
  (optional)

Overview

Players attempt to reach the bottom row of the 120 Chart by finding patterns in the chart (e.g., 10 more, 10 less, 1 more, 1 less).

Objective

Use place value understanding and properties of operations to add and subtract (mentally find 10 more or 10 less).

Procedure

1. Distribute copies of the *120 Chart* activity sheet (page 179; 120chart.pdf) and other materials to students.

2. Players place game markers on any space in the top row.

3. Taking turns, each player spins the spinner and moves his or her playing piece on the chart. For example, if a player is on 24 and spins *10 more*, the player may move 10 spaces on the chart by moving his or her playing piece down one row.

4. The first player to reach the bottom row wins.

5. Players may record their moves in a math journal or on a recording sheet using the sentence stems from the Talking Points card (e.g., *Ten more than 29 is 39.*).

Differentiation

Provide base-ten blocks for **below-level learners** who need concrete support. This also allows students to practice regrouping. For example, if a student is on 20 and spins 1 less, he or she would need to trade a ten for 10 ones to subtract one.

Use charts with larger numbers (e.g., 200–320 or 300–420) for **above-level learners** who are ready to work with a wider range of numbers.

Race to the Bottom

Be the first to reach the bottom row of the *120 Chart!*

120 Chart

1	2	3	4	5	6	7	8	9	10
11	12	13	14	15	16	17	18	19	20
21	22	23	24	25	26	27	28	29	30
31	32	33	34	35	36	37	38	39	40
41	42	43	44	45	46	47	48	49	50
51	52	53	54	55	56	57	58	59	60
61	62	63	64	65	66	67	68	69	70
71	72	73	74	75	76	77	78	79	80
81	82	83	84	85			90
91	92	93	94			100
101	102	103	104		
111	112	113	114		

Spinner sections: 1 less, 1 more, 10 more, 10 less

Materials

- *120 Chart*
- paper clip and pencil
- game markers
- *Race to the Bottom Spinner*
- base-ten blocks (optional)

Directions

1. Place your game marker on any space in the first row.

2. Take turns:
  - Spin the spinner.
  - If you spin *10 less* when you are on the first row, spin again.
  - Move your playing piece.
  - Explain your move. For example, "Ten more than 24 is 34."

3. Reach the bottom row first to win!

Talking Points

Vocabulary

- column
- row
- pattern
- one more →
- one less ←
- ten more ↓
- ten less ↑

Talk like a mathematician:

Ten more than _____ is _____.

Ten less than _____ is _____.

One more than _____ is _____.

One less than _____ is _____.

A pattern I see is _____.

Talking Points

Vocabulary

- column
- row
- pattern
- one more →
- one less ←
- ten more ↓
- ten less ↑

Talk like a mathematician:

Ten more than _____ is _____.

Ten less than _____ is _____.

One more than _____ is _____.

One less than _____ is _____.

A pattern I see is _____.

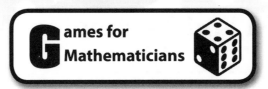

Area and Perimeter War: Grades 3–5

Materials

- *Area and Perimeter War Cards* (pages 181–184; areacards.pdf)
- *Area/Perimeter Spinner* (page 185; areaspinner.pdf)
- paper clip and pencil
- square tiles (optional)

Overview

Players spin the spinner to determine whether they are comparing area or perimeter. Then, they flip over two cards, and the player with the greatest area or perimeter (depending on the spin) wins both cards.

Objective

Understand concepts of area and relate area to multiplication and to addition. Recognize perimeter as an attribute of plane figures and distinguish between linear and area measures.

Procedure

Note: Prior to introducing the workstation task, copy the *Area and Perimeter War Cards* (pages 181–184; areacards.pdf) and *Area/Perimeter Spinner* (page 185; areaspinner.pdf) on cardstock, cut, and laminate.

1. Distribute materials to players.

2. Players divide the cards equally.

3. For each hand, players spin the spinner to determine whether they are comparing area or perimeter.

4. Players turn over their top card and compare the area or perimeter of their shapes, as indicated on the spinner.

5. The player with the greatest area or perimeter wins both cards. The player with the most cards at the end of the game wins.

6. Students may record the result of each hand in a math journal or on a recording sheet. Or, students may write a journal entry explaining the difference between area and perimeter.

Differentiation

For **below-level learners** who need concrete support, provide square tiles for students to build the shapes.

Challenge **above-level learners** to not only determine which area/perimeter is greater, but also find the difference.

Chapter 5

Area and Perimeter War

Collect the most cards by comparing the area or perimeter of the shapes on the cards.

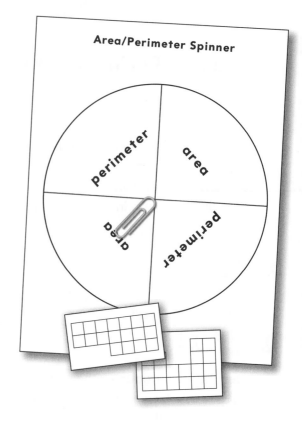

Materials

- *Area and Perimeter War Cards*
- *Area/Perimeter Spinner*
- paper clip and pencil (for spinner)
- square tiles (optional)

Directions

1. Decide which player will go first.

2. Deal an equal number of cards to each player.

3. Spin the spinner to determine whether players will compare area or perimeter.

4. Both players turn over their top card and find the area or perimeter (depending on the spin) of their shape.

5. The player with the greatest area or perimeter wins both cards.

6. Spin the spinner again and repeat.

7. Collect the most cards to win the game!

Talking Points

Vocabulary

- **area**
  (square units covering an object)

- **perimeter**
  (distance around an object)

- **rectangle**

- **square**

- **square units**

Talk like a mathematician:

To find perimeter, I _____ .

To find area, I _____ .

Area is different from perimeter because _____ .

Area is expressed in square units because _____ .

Talking Points

Vocabulary

- **area**
  (square units covering an object)

- **perimeter**
  (distance around an object)

- **rectangle**

- **square**

- **square units**

Talk like a mathematician:

To find perimeter, I _____ .

To find area, I _____ .

Area is different from perimeter because _____ .

Area is expressed in square units because _____ .

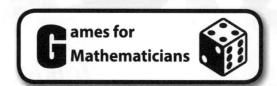

Games for
Mathematicians

Integer Tug-of-War: Grades 6–8

Materials
- 1 game marker
- *Add/Subtract Spinner* (page 186; addspinner.pdf)
- paper clip and pencil
- *Integer Tug-of-War Game Board* (page 187; integergame.pdf)
- standard playing cards (ace–9 only)
- *Recording Sheet* (Grades 6–8) (optional) (recording68.pdf)

Overview

Players add and subtract positive and negative numbers to move the same playing piece back and forth, trying to be the first to reach their home space.

Objectives

Apply and extend previous understandings of numbers to the system of rational numbers by adding and subtracting integers.

Procedure

Note: Prior to introducing the workstation task, copy the *Add/Subtract Spinner* (page 186; addspinner.pdf) and the *Integer Tug-of-War Game Board* (page 187; integergame.pdf) on cardstock and laminate.

1. Distribute materials to students.

2. Players decide who will be Player 1 and Player 2 and place the game marker on the 0 space. Both players use the same playing piece.

3. Players shuffle the cards, and place them facedown in a pile. Red suits (hearts and diamonds) represent negative numbers, and black suits (spades and clubs) represent positive numbers.

4. On each turn, players turn over the top card and move that many spaces toward their home space, spin the *Add/Subtract Spinner*, and create an equation using the number on the game board, the operation on the spinner, and the number on the card.

5. The first player to reach a home space wins.

6. Students may write their equations in a math journal or on a recording sheet.

Differentiation

Have **below-level learners** play the game without the spinner to practice adding integers until they are ready to incorporate subtracting integers.

Instruct **above-level learners** to spin the spinner twice and turn over two cards on each turn to add or subtract three integers.

Chapter 5

Integer Tug-of-War

Be the first player to reach your home space.

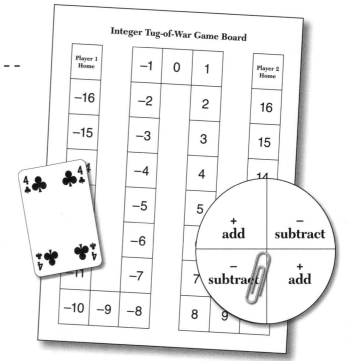

Materials

- 1 game marker
- *Add/Subtract Spinner*
- paper clip and pencil
- *Integer Tug-of-War Game Board*
- standard playing cards (ace–9 only)
- *Recording Sheet* (optional)

Directions

1. Decide who will be Player 1 and Player 2.

2. Shuffle the cards, and place them facedown.

3. Place the game marker on the space marked 0. (Both players use the same game marker.)

4. Take turns:
   - Turn over the top card and move that many spaces toward your home space.
   - Spin the spinner and write an equation using the number on the game board, the operation on the spinner, and the number on the card. (Red cards represent negative numbers and black cards represent positive numbers.)
   - Solve the equation.

5. Be the first to reach your home space to win!

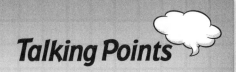

Talking Points

Vocabulary

- integer
- positive number
- negative number
- opposite

Talk like a mathematician:

Subtracting a negative number is like adding a positive number because _____.

The opposite of _____ is _____.

A number line is a useful model for adding and subtracting integers because _____.

A pattern I notice when adding integers is _____.

 ....

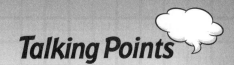

Talking Points

Vocabulary

- integer
- positive number
- negative number
- opposite

Talk like a mathematician:

Subtracting a negative number is like adding a positive number because _____.

The opposite of _____ is _____.

A number line is a useful model for adding and subtracting integers because _____.

A pattern I notice when adding integers is _____.

Using What We Know

Polygon Pictures: Grades K–2

Materials

- *My Polygon Picture* (page 188; polygonpic.pdf)
- pattern blocks
- digital device (optional)

Overview

Students explore with pattern blocks to create a picture or pattern and describe the attributes of the shapes they used.

Objectives

Reason with shapes and their attributes.

Procedure

Note: Students should be given time to freely explore the pattern blocks prior to placing this task in a workstation.

1. Distribute copies of the *My Polygon Picture* activity sheet (page 188; polygonpic.pdf) and other materials to students.

2. Students should know that each piece in the pattern block set is a polygon because it is a closed shape with straight sides and that each piece also has a more specific name. Students should discuss the names and attributes of each pattern block piece.

3. Students use pattern blocks to create pictures or patterns.

4. Students trace their pictures on paper or take photographs of them.

5. Students write the number of each type of block they used and write a number sentence to show the total number of blocks.

6. Students write three sentences describing the attributes of the polygons they used.

7. Students may draw their picture in a math journal or on a recording sheet. Or, students may take a photograph of their picture using a digital device.

Differentiation

Instruct **below-level learners** on the number of blocks they may use to limit the numbers they work with (e.g., numbers to 10).

Have **above-level learners** try to recreate pictures using different pieces (e.g., hexagon can be made with two trapezoids).

Polygon Pictures

Make a picture or pattern using pattern blocks. Count and write the number of blocks you used.

Name: _____

My Polygon Picture

Write the number of blocks you used.

triangles _____   rhombuses _____   trapezoids _____

hexagons _____   squares _____

Number sentence: _____

Describe the attributes of your polygons.

1. _____

_____

2. _____

_____

3. _____

_____

Materials

- *My Polygon Picture*
- pattern blocks
- digital device (optional)

Directions

1. Use the pattern blocks to make a picture or pattern.

2. Trace your picture on paper and color it, or take a photo of it.

3. Count and write the number of blocks you used.

4. Write a number sentence to show how many blocks you used.

5. Write three sentences to tell about the attributes of your polygons.

Talking Points

Vocabulary

- polygon
- attribute
- hexagon ⬡
- rhombus ▱
- square ☐
- triangle △
- trapezoid ⏢

Talk like a mathematician:

The attributes of a _____ are _____.
                    (shape)

A _____ is a polygon because _____.
   (shape)

One way a _____ and a _____ are
            (shape)   (shape)

the same is _____.

✂ -

Talking Points

Vocabulary

- polygon
- attribute
- hexagon ⬡
- rhombus ▱
- square ☐
- triangle △
- trapezoid ⏢

Talk like a mathematician:

The attributes of a _____ are _____.
                    (shape)

A _____ is a polygon because _____.
   (shape)

One way a _____ and a _____ are
            (shape)   (shape)

the same is _____.

Using What We Know

$1,000 House: Grades 3–5

Overview

Students use base-ten blocks to construct a house "worth" $1,000.

Objectives

Generalize place value understanding for multi-digit whole numbers.

Procedure

Note: For this activity, the base-ten blocks have the following values:

- flat = 100
- rod = 10
- unit = 1

1. Distribute materials to students.

2. Using base-ten blocks, students construct a house with a value of $1,000.

3. Students draw pictorial representations of the materials they used for their houses and the values.

4. Students may use digital devices to photograph their creations.

5. Students may show their thinking in a math journal or on a recording sheet.

Differentiation

Change the targeted value of the house to differentiate this activity for **above-level learners** and **below-level learners**.

$1,000 House

Build a house worth exactly $1,000.

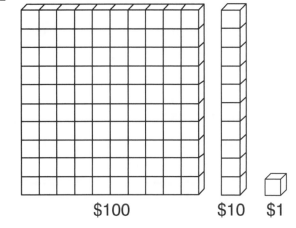

$100 $10 $1

Materials

- base-ten blocks
- digital device (optional)
- *Recording Sheet* (optional)

Directions

1. Each base-ten piece has the value shown in the picture.

2. Build a house with a value of exactly $1,000.

3. Take a photo of your house (optional).

4. Explain the value of $1,000 in at least two ways.

Talking Points

Vocabulary

- place value
- ones
- tens
- hundreds
- sum
- multiply
- product

Talk like a mathematician:

I can group _____ ones to make a 10.

A ten has the same value as _____ ones.

I can group _____ tens or _____ ones to make a hundred.

The value of a ten is _____ times the value of a one.

The value of a hundred is _____ times the value of a ten.

Talking Points

Vocabulary

- place value
- ones
- tens
- hundreds
- sum
- multiply
- product

Talk like a mathematician:

I can group _____ ones to make a 10.

A ten has the same value as _____ ones.

I can group _____ tens or _____ ones to make a hundred.

The value of a ten is _____ times the value of a one.

The value of a hundred is _____ times the value of a ten.

Using What We Know

Graphing Growing Patterns: Grades 6–8

Overview

Students use tiles to create a growing pattern numerically and visually. Students display their pattern and represent it in three different ways.

Objectives

Apply and extend previous understandings of arithmetic to algebraic expressions.

Procedure

Note: Students use their materials to explore growing patterns. Students may work in pairs to facilitate mathematical conversations. A list of guiding questions is provided on the Student Task card to support discussion.

1. Distribute materials to students.

2. Once students are satisfied with their pattern, they may sketch and describe it on *Centimeter Graph Paper* (centgraph.pdf) or chart paper, or they may create a digital presentation.

Differentiation

To scaffold the learning for this task, provide **below-level learners** with simple patterns to duplicate and describe in multiple ways. Challenge **above-level learners** with a higher-level task by having them create and describe an original pattern.

This task is self-differentiating because students will create more and less complicated patterns.

Graphing Growing Patterns

Create a growing pattern, generalize the pattern, and describe it in multiple ways.

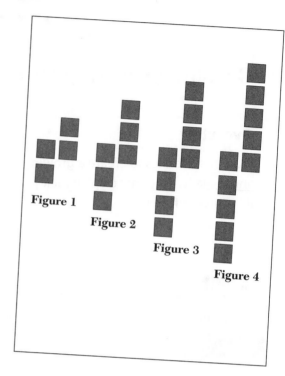

Figure 1

Figure 2

Figure 3

Figure 4

Materials

- *Centimeter Graph Paper* or chart paper
- square tiles, pattern blocks, or cubes

Directions

1. Use square tiles, blocks, or cubes to create a growing pattern. Your pattern should grow both numerically and visually.

2. Consider these questions as you explore and create your pattern:
   - How does your pattern change numerically? Visually?
   - Could you create a different pattern that grows the same way numerically, but not visually?
   - How can you explain in words what is taking place in your pattern?
   - Can you create a generalized rule that would help you find the 100th term?
   - How many different ways can you explain your pattern?

3. Create a display. Include your pattern and at least three different ways to describe and represent it (e.g., describe in words, function table, graph, equation).

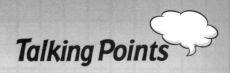

Talking Points

Vocabulary

- function
- generalize
- *y*-value
- *x*-value
- input
- output
- rate of change
- linear function
- non-linear function

Talk like a mathematician:

Representing functions in multiple ways helps

to _____.

I can generalize my pattern by _____.

Functions can be used to solve problems by _____.

My pattern can/cannot be represented by a linear equation because _____.

Talking Points

Vocabulary

- function
- generalize
- *y*-value
- *x*-value
- input
- output
- rate of change
- linear function
- non-linear function

Talk like a mathematician:

Representing functions in multiple ways helps

to _____.

I can generalize my pattern by _____.

Functions can be used to solve problems by _____.

My pattern can/cannot be represented by a linear equation because _____.

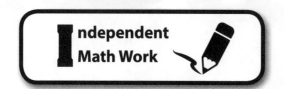

Piggy Bank Problems: Grades K–2

Materials

- *Piggy Bank Problems Cards* (page 189; piggycard.pdf)

- *What's the Value?* (pages 190–191; whatvalue.pdf)

- *Coin Value Chart* (optional) (page 192; coinvalue.pdf)

- play coins

- *120 Chart* (optional) (page 179; 120chart.pdf)

Overview

Students draw five cards and find the value of the collection of coins shown on the cards.

Objectives

Find the value of a collection of coins.

Procedure

Note: Prior to introducing the workstation task, copy the *Piggy Bank Problems Cards* (page 189; piggycard.pdf) on cardstock, cut, and laminate.

1. Distribute copies of the *What's the Value?* activity sheet (pages 190–191; whatvalue.pdf) and other materials to students.

2. Students draw five cards, arrange them by like coins from greatest value to least value, and find the value of the coins. Using one set of cards, the value of the collection will always be under one dollar. Students may use play money or the *120 Chart* (page 179; 120chart.pdf) to help them count.

3. Students record the five coins from the cards and the value of the collection, using both the cent symbol and a dollar sign and decimal point, on the recording sheet.

4. Students continue with five more cards, reshuffling and reusing the cards as needed.

5. Students may turn in the *What's the Value?* activity sheet or glue it in a math journal.

Differentiation

Copy the *Coin Value Chart* (page 192; coinvalue.pdf) on cardstock, cut, and laminate. Have **below-level learners** who need support lay the coin value pieces over the *120 Chart* to determine the value of the collection.

Challenge **above-level learners** with the following ideas:

- Make several copies of the cards and allow students to draw more cards, creating the possibility of collections over one dollar.

- Have students find one or more additional ways to create the same value using different coins.

- Have students list the values of their coin collections from least to greatest or greatest to least.

Piggy Bank Problems

Find the value of a collection of coins.

Materials

- *Piggy Bank Problems* Cards
- *What's the Value?*
- *Coin Value Chart* (optional)
- play coins
- *120 Chart* (optional)

Directions

1. Shuffle the cards and put them facedown in a pile.

2. Draw 5 cards.

3. Arrange the cards so like coins are together. Arrange the groups from greatest value to least value.

4. Find the value of the coins. Use play coins or the *120 Chart* to help you.

5. Show your thinking on the *What's the Value?* activity sheet.

Talking Points

Vocabulary	Talk like a mathematician:
• quarter (25¢) • dime (10¢) • nickel (5¢) • penny (1¢) • cent • value	My strategy for finding the value of the coins is _____. The value of my coins is _____. Another way to show the same amount is _____. I arranged my coins from greatest value to least value because _____.

✂ ┄┄┄┄┄┄┄┄┄┄┄┄┄┄┄┄┄┄┄┄┄┄┄┄┄┄┄┄┄┄┄┄┄┄┄┄

Talking Points

Vocabulary	Talk like a mathematician:
• quarter (25¢) • dime (10¢) • nickel (5¢) • penny (1¢) • cent • value	My strategy for finding the value of the coins is _____. The value of my coins is _____. Another way to show the same amount is _____. I arranged my coins from greatest value to least value because _____.

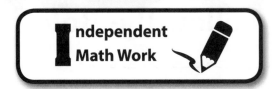

Independent Math Work

Follow the Rule: Grades 3–5

Overview

Given an addition or multiplication rule, students will add or multiply numbers in the input column to find the numbers in the output column.

Objectives

Generate additive and multiplicative number patterns using an input-output table and a given rule.

Materials

- *Rule Cards* (pages 193–194; rulecard.pdf)
- *Input-Output Cards* (pages 195–196; inoutcard.pdf)
- *Follow the Rule Recording Sheet* (page 197; followrecord.pdf)
- *Follow the Rule Graphing Sheet* (optional) (page 198; followgraph.pdf)

Procedure

Note: Prior to introducing the workstation task, copy the *Rule Cards* (pages 193–194; rulecard.pdf) and *Input-Output Cards* (pages 195–196; inoutcard.pdf) on cardstock, cut, and laminate. Consider copying each set of cards on a different color to make organizing the cards for play easier.

1. Distribute copies of the *Follow the Rule Recording Sheet* (page 197; followrecord.pdf) and other materials to students.

2. Students place the *Rule Cards* and *Input-Output Cards* facedown in two piles.

3. Students turn over one *Rule Card* and one *Input-Output Card*. They copy the rule in one section of the *Follow the Rule Recording Sheet* and write the numbers in the input column. There is one additional space for students to add their own input number.

4. Students apply the rule and write the result in the output column.

5. Students repeat with three additional cards.

6. Students may turn in the *Follow the Rule Recording Sheet* or glue it in a math journal.

Differentiation

Provide an addition and multiplication chart for **below-level learners**.

Have **above-level learners** write a formula for the rule using the variables x and y, and graph the pattern on the *Follow the Rule Graphing Sheet* (page 198; followgraph.pdf).

Another option for extending this task is to have students write real-life scenarios for one of the rules.

Chapter 5

Follow the Rule

Generate addition and multiplication patterns using an input-output table and a given rule.

Materials

- *Rule Cards*
- *Input-Output Cards*
- *Follow the Rule Recording Sheet*

Directions

1. Place the *Rule Cards* and *Input-Output Cards* facedown in two piles.

2. Turn over one *Rule Card* and one *Input-Output Card*.

3. Write the rule from the *Rule Card* on the *Follow the Rule Recording Sheet*.

4. Write the input numbers from the *Input-Output Card* in the Input column.

5. Write your own input number in the extra space.

6. Apply the rule to the input numbers to find the output numbers.

7. Repeat with 3 more cards.

Talking Points

Vocabulary

- pattern
- addition pattern
- multiplication pattern
- input-output table
- rule

Talk like a mathematician:

This is an addition pattern because _____.

This is a multiplication pattern because _____.

The relationship between the input and output numbers is _____.

A pattern I notice in the output numbers is _____.

Talking Points

Vocabulary

- pattern
- addition pattern
- multiplication pattern
- input-output table
- rule

Talk like a mathematician:

This is an addition pattern because _____.

This is a multiplication pattern because _____.

The relationship between the input and output numbers is _____.

A pattern I notice in the output numbers is _____.

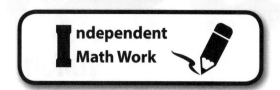

Independent Math Work

Slope and Intercept: Grades 6–8

Overview

Students choose cards with a *y*-intercept and one ordered pair, and graph the line. Then, students find the slope of the line and write the equation in slope-intercept form.

Materials

- *Y-Intercept Cards* (page 199; ycard.pdf)
- *Ordered Pair Cards* (page 200; orderedcard.pdf)
- *Slope and Intercept Recording Sheet* (page 201; sloperecord.pdf)

Objectives

Graph a line, determine the slope of the line, and derive the slope-intercept form.

Procedure

1. Distribute copies of the *Slope and Intercept Recording Sheet* (page 201; sloperecord.pdf) and other materials to students.

2. Students choose a *Y-Intercept Card* (page 199; ycard.pdf) and an *Ordered Pair Card* (page 200; orderedcard.pdf).

3. Using one of the coordinate grids on the *Slope and Intercept Recording Sheet*, students plot the *y*-intercept and the ordered pair and graph the line.

4. Students determine the slope of the line (rise over run).

5. Students use the *y*-intercept and slope to describe the line using slope-intercept form.

6. Students may turn in the *Slope and Intercept Recording Sheet*.

Differentiation

Have **below-level learners** review and practice linear equation concepts online using guided instructional videos.

Instruct **above-level learners** to choose two ordered pair cards, graph the line, and find both the slope and *y*-intercept.

Chapter 5

Slope and Intercept

Graph a line using the *y*-intercept and one ordered pair, find the slope of the line, and write the slope-intercept form for the line.

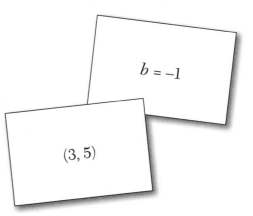

Materials

- *Y-Intercept Cards*
- *Ordered Pair Cards*
- *Slope and Intercept Recording Sheet*

$$\text{Slope} = \frac{\text{rise}}{\text{run}} = \frac{\Delta y}{\Delta x} = \frac{y_2 - y_1}{x_2 - x_1}$$

Slope-intercept form: $y = mx + b$
      m is the slope of the line
      b is the *y*-intercept
The *y*-intercept is the point where the line crosses the *y*-axis.

Directions

1. Choose a *Y-Intercept Card* and an *Ordered Pair Card*.

2. On your *Slope and Intercept Recording Sheet*, plot the *y*-intercept and the ordered pair and graph the line.

3. Determine the slope of the line. Justify your answer using a formula for finding slope.

4. Describe the line using slope-intercept form.

Challenge

Choose two *Ordered Pair Cards*, graph the line, find both the slope and *y*-intercept, and describe the line in slope-intercept form.

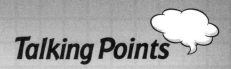

Talking Points

Vocabulary	Talk like a mathematician:

Vocabulary

- linear equation
- *x*-axis
- *y*-axis
- ordered pair
- *y*-intercept
- slope
- slope-intercept form
- rise
- run

Talk like a mathematician:

A pattern I notice on my graph is _____.

Modeling on a graph helps me _____.

The relationship between the graph and the line is _____.

If the slope is negative, I know _____.

A positive slope tells me _____.

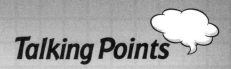

Talking Points

Vocabulary

- linear equation
- *x*-axis
- *y*-axis
- ordered pair
- *y*-intercept
- slope
- slope-intercept form
- rise
- run

Talk like a mathematician:

A pattern I notice on my graph is _____.

Modeling on a graph helps me _____.

The relationship between the graph and the line is _____.

If the slope is negative, I know _____.

A positive slope tells me _____.

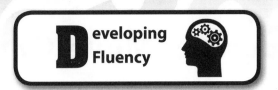

Developing **Fluency**

Addition Move One: Grades K–2

Materials

• *Addition Move One Game Board* (page 202; addgame.pdf)

• 2 paper clips

• dry-erase markers

• *Addition/Subtraction Chart* (optional) (page 203; addsubtract.pdf)

Overview

Students change one addend to capture a space on the game board. The first player to get four in a row wins.

Objectives

Add and subtract within 20 using mental strategies.

Procedure

Note: Prior to introducing the workstation task, copy the *Addition Move One Game Board* (page 202; addgame.pdf) on cardstock (one game board per student pair) and laminate, or place in a sheet protector.

1. Distribute materials to students.

2. Player 1 places the paper clips on two addends at the bottom of the game board, adds to find the sum, and marks a space with the sum on the game board.

3. Player 2 moves only one paper clip to a different addend, adds, and marks a space with the sum on the game board. Both paper clips may be placed on the same addend (e.g., 3 and 3).

4. Players may use X's and O's to differentiate their marks or different color markers.

5. The first player to claim four spaces in a row wins.

6. Students may record the facts from each of their turns in a math journal. Or, students may make a brief video explaining their strategy and reflecting on changes they might try when playing the game again.

Differentiation

Some players are using the game to build automaticity, while others are playing to learn their math facts. Include an *Addition/Subtraction Chart* (page 203; addsubtract.pdf) and encourage students to use the chart rather than guess at a math fact they do not know.

Create a game board with fewer addends for **below-level learners**. For example, create a board game with the addends 0, 1, 2, 3, 4, and 5 to practice only math facts to 5.

Have **above-level learners** combine 3 addends using 3 paper clips.

Addition Move One

Choose addends to mark four spaces in a row on the game board.

Materials

- *Addition Move One Game Board*
- 2 paper clips
- dry-erase markers
- *Addition/Subtraction Chart* (optional)

Addition Move One Game Board

11	18	7	13	8	5	10	16
9	5	12	16	18	14	9	17
8	10	14	6	11	12	13	6
14	11	15	10	15	8	16	11
6	13	9	14	17	12	5	17
17	10	16	5	7	15	16	12
7	14	12	15	18	6	9	18
13	7	18	8	11	17	15	10

2 3 4 5 6 7 8 9

Directions

1. Choose which player will go first.

2. **Player 1**: Place the paper clips on two addends at the bottom of the game board. (Both paper clips may be placed on the same addend.) Add to find the sum. Mark a space with that sum on the game board.
Player 2: Move one paper clip to a different addend. Add to find the sum. Mark a space with that sum on the game board.

3. Play continues until a player marks four spaces in a row to win!

51654—Guided Math Workshop   © Shell Education

Talking Points

Vocabulary

- addend
- sum
- plus
- add
- addition
- double

Talk like a mathematician:

I marked the sum _____ because _____ plus _____ equals _____.

_____ is the sum of _____ and _____.

The addends I chose are _____ and _____ because they have a sum of _____.

The strategy I used to choose my addends is _____.

✂ -

Talking Points

Vocabulary

- addend
- sum
- plus
- add
- addition
- double

Talk like a mathematician:

I marked the sum _____ because _____ plus _____ equals _____.

_____ is the sum of _____ and _____.

The addends I chose are _____ and _____ because they have a sum of _____.

The strategy I used to choose my addends is _____.

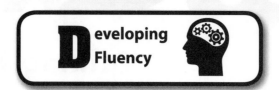

Multiples Tic-Tac-Toe: Grades 3–5

Materials

- *Number Cards* (page 204; numbercards.pdf)

- *Multiples Tic-Tac-Toe Game Board* (page 205; multiplesboard.pdf)

- dry-erase markers in two colors

- *Alternate Number Cards* (optional) (page 206; altcards.pdf)

Overview

Students attempt to claim three spaces in a row on the game board by finding multiples of a given factor.

Objectives

Determine whether a given whole number is a multiple of a given one-digit number.

Procedure

Note: Prior to introducing the workstation task, copy the *Number Cards* (page 204; numbercards.pdf) on cardstock, cut, and laminate.

1. Distribute materials to students.

2. Players place number cards facedown in a pile, turn over the top card, and write the number in the star labeled *Multiples of…* on the *Multiples Tic-Tac-Toe Game Board* (page 205; multiplesboard.pdf).

3. Players decide who will go first. Then, players take turns claiming spaces by multiplying the factor in the star by the factor in the space and writing the product in the space.

4. The first player to claim three spaces in a row wins.

5. Students may record the multiples for each factor in a math journal or on a recording sheet. Students may also explain patterns they notice in the multiples of the numbers.

Differentiation

Have **below-level learners** still learning the concept of multiplication use concrete objects to build each multiple.

Instruct **above-level learners** to use the *Alternate Number Cards* (page 206; altcards.pdf) and work with multiples of ten.

Multiples Tic-Tac-Toe

Claim three spaces in a row on the game board by finding multiples of a given factor.

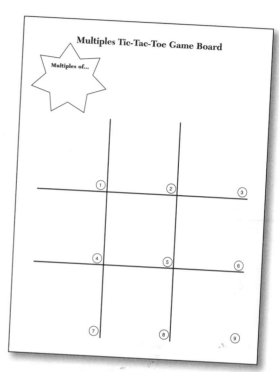

Materials

- *Numbers Cards*
- *Multiples Tic-Tac-Toe Game Board*
- dry-erase markers in two colors

Directions

1. Shuffle the number cards, and place them facedown in a pile.

2. Turn over the top card, and write the number in the star labeled *Multiples of…* on the game board.

3. Decide which player will go first.

4. Take turns claiming spaces on the game board by multiplying the factor in the star by the factor shown in a space. Write the product of the two factors in the same space.

5. Play continues until a player marks three spaces in a row to win!

Talking Points

Vocabulary
- product
- multiply
- factor
- multiple

Talk like a mathematician:

_____ is the product of _____ and _____.

_____ is a multiple of _____.

The strategy I used is _____.

Factors and multiples are related because _____.

A pattern I notice in the multiples of _____ is _____.

Talking Points

Vocabulary
- product
- multiply
- factor
- multiple

Talk like a mathematician:

_____ is the product of _____ and _____.

_____ is a multiple of _____.

The strategy I used is _____.

Factors and multiples are related because _____.

A pattern I notice in the multiples of _____ is _____.

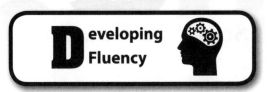

Scientific Notation: Grades 6–8

- -

Overview

Students select cards to convert numbers written in scientific notation to standard form and perform operations with numbers expressed in scientific notation.

- -

Materials

- *Scientific Notation Task Cards* (pages 207–212; sciencetask.pdf)

- *Scientific Notation Recording Sheet* (page 213; sciencerecord.pdf)

- *Scientific Notation Operations Recording Sheet* (optional) (page 214; scienceop.pdf)

- *Operation Cards* (optional) (page 215; opcard.pdf)

Objectives

Use numbers expressed in the form of a single digit multiplied by an integer power of 10 to estimate very large or very small quantities, and perform operations with numbers expressed in scientific notation.

Procedure

Note: Prior to introducing the workstation task, copy the *Scientific Notation Task Cards* (pages 207–212; sciencetask.pdf) on cardstock, cut, and laminate.

1. Distribute copies of the *Scientific Notation Recording Sheet* (page 213; sciencerecord.pdf) and other materials to students.

2. Some or all task cards may be used at one time. For example, you might only use the cards for converting from scientific notation to standard form or only the cards for converting from standard form to scientific notation before using all the task cards.

3. Students choose up to 10 cards and record both the standard form and scientific notation on the *Scientific Notation Recording Sheet*.

4. An optional *Scientific Notation Operations Recording Sheet* (page 214; scienceop.pdf) and *Operation Cards* (page 215; opcard.pdf) are included to provide practice on performing operations with numbers expressed in scientific notation.

5. Students may turn in the *Scientific Notation Recording Sheets*.

Differentiation

Scaffold learning for **below-level learners** who have difficulty with this task by preparing cards with less complex numbers, building up to the numbers provided in this task. For example, use numbers such as 5×10^3 or 0.075.

Challenge **above-level learners** to find real-life examples of very small or very large numbers and express the numbers in scientific notation.

Scientific Notation

Task 1: Convert between scientific notation and standard form to express very small and very large numbers.

Task 2: Perform operations with numbers expressed in scientific notation.

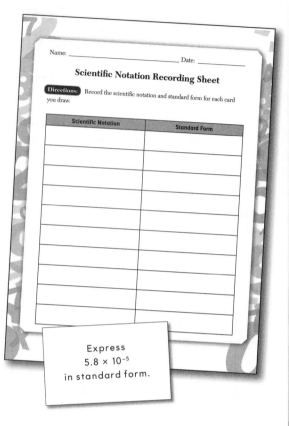

Materials

- *Scientific Notation Task Cards*
- *Scientific Notation Recording Sheet*
- *Scientific Notation Operations Recording Sheet* (optional)
- *Operation Cards* (optional)

Directions

Task 1:

1. Choose 1 *Scientific Notation Task Card*.

2. Follow the directions on the card, and record your calculations on the *Scientific Notation Recording Sheet*.

Task 2:

1. Choose 6 *Scientific Notation Task Cards*.

2. Use the 6 cards and the *Operation Cards* to create 1 addition problem, 1 multiplication problem, and 1 subtraction problem.

3. Show your solutions on the *Scientific Notation Operations Recording Sheet*.

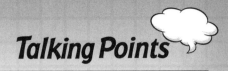

Talking Points

Vocabulary

- exponent
- base number
- power
- scientific notation
- standard form

Talk like a mathematician:

Scientific notation is helpful when working with very small or very large numbers because _____.

I can convert a number from standard form to scientific notation by _____.

I can change a number written in standard form to scientific notation by _____.

A negative exponent means that _____.

Talking Points

Vocabulary

- exponent
- base number
- power
- scientific notation
- standard form

Talk like a mathematician:

Scientific notation is helpful when working with very small or very large numbers because _____.

I can convert a number from standard form to scientific notation by _____.

I can change a number written in standard form to scientific notation by _____.

A negative exponent means that _____.

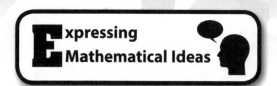

Expressing Mathematical Ideas

Math Vocabulary Book: Grades K–2

Overview

Students define and illustrate math words in a personal vocabulary book.

Objectives

Communicate precisely, using clear definitions when discussing and reasoning about mathematics.

Procedure

Note: Prior to introducing the workstation task, assemble a *Math Vocabulary Book* for each student. Each double-sided vocabulary page accommodates four words.

1. Distribute the copies of the *My Math Vocabulary Book* (pages 216–218; mathvocab.pdf) and other materials to students.

2. Students use the cover provided to create a math vocabulary book that may be used all year long, or they may create an alternate cover for topic-specific vocabulary books.

3. Students will either choose or be assigned a mathematical word.

4. Students complete a page of the book as follows:
   • **Word**—vocabulary word
   • **What it means**—student definition of the word
   • **What it looks like**—drawing showing the vocabulary word

5. Consider having students record their definition as an audio file, generate a QR code, and glue the code in the "What It Means" section.

6. Students may turn in the *My Math Vocabulary Books*.

Differentiation

Provide words and definitions that may be cut and pasted for **below-level learners** who struggle with writing and defining the vocabulary words. They may show their understanding of the words by creating illustrations or by using a voice recorder to record the definition in their own words.

Have **above-level learners** create books using the Alternate *My Math Vocabulary Book* (pages 219–221; altvocab.pdf) version of the vocabulary pages, which includes a "Reminds Me Of" section for making connections.

Materials

• *My Math Vocabulary Book* (pages 216–218; mathvocab.pdf)

• crayons or colored pencils (optional)

• Math Word Wall or list of vocabulary words

• digital device for recording an audio of the definition (optional)

• Alternate *My Math Vocabulary Book* (pages 219–221; altvocab.pdf)

Math Vocabulary Book

Tell about words and show their meanings.

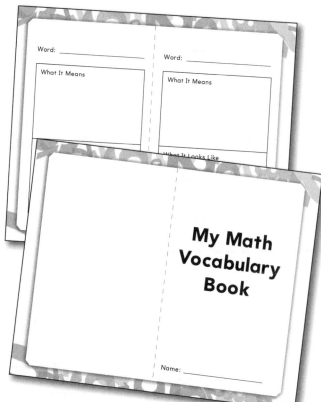

Materials

- *My Math Vocabulary Book*
- crayons or colored pencils (optional)

Directions

1. Think about what the math word means and what it looks like.

2. Turn to the next blank page in your book.

3. In each part of the chart:
   - **Word**: Write the math vocabulary word.
   - **What It Means**: Explain what the word means.
   - **What It Looks Like**: Draw a picture to show what the word means.

4. Remember to use precise mathematical language.

Talking Points

Vocabulary

- explain
- describe
- represent
- example
- non-example
- connection

Talk like a mathematician:

The word _____ means _____.

My picture represents _____.

The word _____ reminds me of _____.

An example of _____ is _____.

An non-example of _____ is _____.

I made a connection between _____ and _____ because _____.

Talking Points

Vocabulary

- explain
- describe
- represent
- example
- non-example
- connection

Talk like a mathematician:

The word _____ means _____.

My picture represents _____.

The word _____ reminds me of _____.

An example of _____ is _____.

An non-example of _____ is _____.

I made a connection between _____ and _____ because _____.

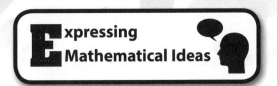

Expressing Mathematical Ideas

This Reminds Me Of...: Grades 3–5

Overview

Students analyze a picture of a model and make mathematical connections, by looking for details, patterns, and relationships.

Materials

- *Mathematical Models* (pages 222–223; mathmodels.pdf)
- glue or tape
- *This Reminds Me Of... Recording Sheet* (page 224; remindsme.pdf)
- student photographs (optional)

Objectives

Recognize connections between mathematical concepts and use precise language to communicate relationships.

Procedure

Note: Prior to introducing the workstation task, copy and cut the *Mathematical Models* (pages 222–223; mathmodels.pdf) into strips. Look through other teaching resources to find additional mathematical models.

1. Distribute copies of the *This Reminds Me Of... Recording Sheet* (page 224; remindsme.pdf) and other materials to students.

2. Students choose a strip with a picture of a model, glue or tape it in the space just below "This Reminds Me Of…" on the recording sheet, and describe their connection. For example, a number line with markings between the whole numbers should create a connection to fractions. A picture showing equal groups should trigger a connection to either multiplication or division. Likewise, students might make a connection between a picture of base-ten blocks and place value.

3. Create a display using student photographs along with their *This Reminds Me Of… Recording Sheets*.

4. Students may turn in the *This Reminds Me Of… Recording Sheets*.

Differentiation

For **below-level learners**, provide a choice of several concepts that may be related to the picture and let them choose one. For example, you might give students a card with the words *addition*, *multiplication*, and *fractions* to accompany a model. They may choose the word they think has a connection to the model and then write an explanation.

Have **above-level learners** write a story problem related to the model.

This Reminds Me Of...

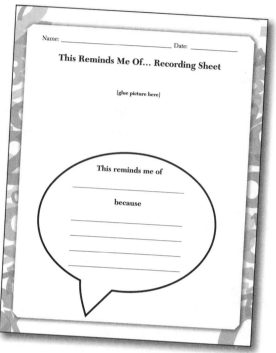

Analyze a model and make mathematical connections.

Materials

- *Mathematical Models*
- glue or tape
- *This Reminds Me Of... Recording Sheet*

Directions

1. Choose a mathematical model, and glue or tape it on your recording sheet in the space labeled "glue picture here."

2. Carefully observe your model like a mathematician, looking for details, patterns, and relationships. What do you notice? What does it remind you of? Be sure to spend enough time on this step.

3. Complete your recording sheet as follows:
   - This reminds me of—What mathematical concept does this picture make you think of?
   - Because—What is it about the picture that creates that connection?

4. Remember to use precise mathematical language.

Talking Points

Vocabulary
- connection
- notice
- observe
- pattern
- diagram
- model
- justify

Talk like a mathematician:

This model reminds me of _____ because _____.

I noticed _____.

_____ and _____ are related because _____.

I made a connection between _____ and _____ because _____.

✂ ....

Talking Points

Vocabulary
- connection
- notice
- observe
- pattern
- diagram
- model
- justify

Talk like a mathematician:

This model reminds me of _____ because _____.

I noticed _____.

_____ and _____ are related because _____.

I made a connection between _____ and _____ because _____.

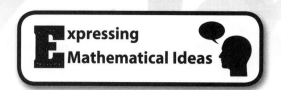

Making Connections: Grades 6–8

Materials

- 2 number cubes
- *Making Connections Vocabulary Board* (page 225; connectboard.pdf)
- *Making Connections Graphic Organizer* (page 226; connectorg.pdf)
- *Compare-and-Contrast Graphic Organizer* (optional) (page 227; compareorg.pdf)

Overview

Students roll two number cubes to choose a vocabulary word and describe personal connections, math connections, and real-world connections to the word.

Objectives

Make sense of math by formulating personal, mathematical, and real-world connections to mathematical concepts.

Procedure

1. Distribute copies of the *Making Connections Graphic Organizer* (page 226; connectorg.pdf) and other materials to students.

2. Students roll two number cubes and find the space where the two numbers intersect on the *Making Connections Vocabulary Board* (page 225; connectboard.pdf). This gives the student a choice of two words. For example, a roll of 1 and 3 could be used as column 1 and row 3 or column 3 and row 1.

3. Students complete the *Making Connections Graphic Organizer* to describe connections to that vocabulary word.

   - **My connections**—Students describe personal connections to the vocabulary term. A student's connections to *percent*, for example, might be the grade they earned on a quiz.

   - **Math connections**—Students describe connections to other math concepts. A math connection for *percent* might be a connection to fractions or decimals.

   - **Real-world connections**—Students describe ways in which they might see this math concept in everyday life. An example would be the connection between *percent* and the savings during a sale at a clothing store.

4. Students may turn in their *Making Connections Graphic Organizers*.

Differentiation

Support **below-level learners** by creating graphic organizers with some of the connections filled in. Provide them with a word bank (or use the *Making Connections Vocabulary Board*), and have them complete the *Making Connections Graphic Organizer*.

Have **above-level learners** use both words from the roll, complete the *Making Connections Graphic Organizer* for both, and compare and contrast the two words using the *Compare-and-Contrast Graphic Organizer* (page 227; compareorg.pdf).

Making Connections

Describe connections to a math
vocabulary word.

Materials

- *Making Connections Vocabulary Board*
- *Making Connections Graphic Organizer*

Directions

1. Roll 2 number cubes and find the space where the row and column intersects. For example, a roll of 1 and 3 could be used as column 1 and row 3 (*ordered pair*) or column 3 and row 1 (*integer*).

2. Write your word or phrase in the space marked *Word* on the *Making Connections Graphic Organizer*.

3. Think carefully about connections you have to the vocabulary word. Connections may be one of three types:
   - **My connections**—*What personal connections do you have with the word?*
   - **Math connections**—*What other math concepts have a connection to this vocabulary word?*
   - **Real-world connections**—*What does this math concept look like in everyday life?*

4. Complete the rest of the graphic organizer. Remember to use precise mathematical language.

Making Connections Vocabulary Board

	1	2	3	4	5	6
1	area	factor	integer	variable	distributive property	statistics
2	circumference	rational number	right triangle	absolute value	rate	prism
3	ordered pair	equation	spread	quadrant	quadrilateral	polygon
4	probability	percent	inequality	evaluate	protractor	population
5	scale	pyramid	coefficient	ratio	tree diagram	random sample
6	obtuse triangle	supplementary angles	volume	frequency	volume	coordinate plane

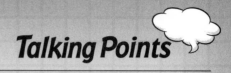

Talking Points

Vocabulary

- connection
- reflect
- research
- discuss
- notice
- reason

Talk like a mathematician:

The word _____ reminds me of _____ because _____.

I made a connection between _____ and _____ because _____.

This connection is important because _____.

I can relate the word _____ to _____ because _____.

Talking Points

Vocabulary

- connection
- reflect
- research
- discuss
- notice
- reason

Talk like a mathematician:

The word _____ reminds me of _____ because _____.

I made a connection between _____ and _____ because _____.

This connection is important because _____.

I can relate the word _____ to _____ because _____.

Review and Reflect

1. What do you notice about these tasks? Are they similar to the kinds of student tasks you use in your classroom? How are they similar or different?

2. In what ways do these tasks support independent student work?

3. How can you modify the resources you already have for use in math workstations?

51654—Guided Math Workshop

Implementing Math Workshop

The secret to success in managing Math Workshop is careful preparation. Once you develop a set of routines and procedures, share them with your students. Unless they know your expectations for Math Workshop behavior, they can't possibly meet them. Allow ample time for students to practice before moving into full Math Workshop mode. The goal during the first few weeks of Math Workshop is to create a learning culture in which students know and apply routines and procedures and are ready to assume the responsibility for their mathematical learning.

Strategies for Teaching Routines and Procedures

During the first 15 days, teach students what is expected of them during Math Workshop, and give them many opportunities to practice. Incorporate the strategies listed below to implement this plan.

Introduce and Practice Routines and Procedures

To truly *know* and *understand* behavioral expectations for working independently, students must see behaviors modeled. Follow these steps to introduce Math Workshop routines and procedures to students during the first 15 days of Math Workshop. At any time throughout the year, if you modify the routines and procedures or if your students need a reminder of the expectations for Math Workshop, revisit these steps.

1. Introduce a routine or procedure. Be as specific as possible in describing it.

2. Model the desired behavior for students. Ask students what they observed. *What did you see? How did it look? How did it sound?* Record student responses on an anchor chart for their future reference.

3. Next, model the behavior done incorrectly. Ask students what they observed. *What did you see this time? How did it look? How did it sound? How was it different from the first time? How do you think these differences affect my work and the work of the class?* During the discussion, refer back to the anchor chart. Ensure that students understand how the routines and procedures should be carried out and how the incorrect behavior impacts the class as a whole.

4. Have several students role-play the routine or procedure as it should look and sound if done properly. Again, ask students to share what they observed. *How does this behavior help us as a class during Math Workshop? How does it help us learn?*

5. Ask several students to role-play the behavior done incorrectly. Review the anchor chart. Ask students what they observed. *How is the modeled behavior different from what is on the anchor chart? How can it be changed to meet expectations?*

6. Provide students with plenty of practice sessions, each followed with self-reflection by the class on what they did well and in what ways they could do better, as well as reflecting on your feedback.

Monitor student behavior during Math Workshop throughout the year to be certain students understand workshop fundamentals. Diller (2011) suggests that students must know how to:

➡ use materials and equipment properly

➡ share materials with other students at workstations

➡ take turns when playing games or sharing resources

➡ decide what tasks to work on at workstations

➡ solve any problems that may arise

➡ put the workstation materials away properly

➡ make transitions

If you find that students are having difficulty with any of these topics, address the issue(s) with either the particular students involved or with the whole class, depending upon your observations.

Practice to Build Student Stamina

Just as building stamina has become standard procedure for preparing students for literacy workshops, it is also essential for preparing students for a successful Math Workshop (Boushey and Moser 2006). Students need multiple opportunities to practice working independently to build stamina.

Begin by having learners work independently for just a short period of time—perhaps five minutes. Call the group back together after the practice session to assess how well they did. Ask them to rate their behavior as compared to the kinds of behaviors described on the anchor chart previously created (see Week 1 of The First 15 Days on page 134). What specifically did they do well? What could they do to improve their behavior when working independently? Following the debrief session, have them practice working independently again. Repeat this process as often as needed, each time gradually increasing the length of time to build stamina. Once students demonstrate ability to follow routines and procedures, it is time to launch Math Workshop.

By following these steps, you provide valuable scaffolding for students to help them assume responsibility for their own behavior. Although time consuming, the process teaches students how to be successful independent learners and, in turn, creates an environment in which conducting small-group instruction and math conferences is possible.

Provide Timely and Specific Feedback

To be most effective, it is important that students receive *timely* and *specific* feedback. This lets them know precisely what it is they are doing well and how they can improve their performance. It may come from whole-class reflection and self-assessment or directly from the teacher based on routines and procedures students have learned.

Expecting learners to self-assess encourages them to more carefully reflect on their own work habits and those of the class, comparing their behavior to the descriptions of exemplary behavior recorded on anchor charts. These experiences deepen student understanding of responsibilities when working independently.

Strategies for Introducing Math Workstation Tasks

During the first 15 days, students learn the Math Workshop basics. Refrain from introducing specific Math Workstation tasks until students understand what Math Workshop is and why it is important for their learning. They should also know the nuts and bolts of how it operates—where workspaces are located, where workstations are stored, what they should do with a workstation task, how to use Talking Points cards, and how to work independently during Math Workshop. Do not assume that devoting 15 days to preparing students for Math Workshop will leave them completely equipped. As specific workstation tasks are introduced throughout the year, students will need ongoing review of these aspects of Math Workshop.

Devote sufficient time to introducing new workstation tasks. Although there never seems to be enough time for math instruction, avoid the temptation to cut corners when introducing workstation tasks to students. Help them understand both *what* the tasks involve and *why* they are important mathematically before they begin their work. Luckily, since workstation tasks are not changed as often with the GUIDE workshop structure as with many other workshop models, less time is required for the introduction of tasks within this model.

The inclusion of games or materials used previously by students in lessons as workstation tasks makes Math Workshop run more efficiently in several ways. With those tasks, students already have a good idea of what they are expected to do (although students may need at least a brief review of the task and its requirements). Moreover, since those materials and games have already been prepared, little prep time is required. And, they provide valuable distributive practice that leads students to develop deeper understanding and retain their mastery of the content.

The goal of introducing Math Workstation tasks is to help students understand them as quickly as possible. The faster they understand the task, the faster they may engage with the task.

Follow these steps when introducing Math Workstation tasks to your class:

1. **Share the purpose of the task.** People have an innate need to know why they are engaged in the work that they do. According to Boushey and Moser (2006, 22), "when people understand a reason for a task, it establishes motivation and becomes a force that keeps them persevering." When students truly understand the mathematical connections behind workstation tasks, they are much more likely to achieve the instructional objectives.

With this understanding, student engagement with tasks becomes more than simply going through procedural motions and following directions. Instead, students learn to think about and monitor their own learning. A word of caution, however—teachers should not be so explicit that they deprive students of opportunities to construct mathematical meaning during Math Workshop. For instance, if a task is designed to help students discover Pythagoras's Theorem, let them know they will be learning about the relationship between the sides of a right triangle rather than telling them they will learn that the square of the hypotenuse is equal to the sum of the squares of the other two sides. Give learners the responsibility to think, observe, struggle, and ultimately make sense of the math with which they are working. In this way, you play an enormous role in helping students engage in metacognitive processes that lead them to a deeper understanding by reflecting on what they are learning about the discipline of mathematics.

This introductory step is teacher-centered. Resist the temptation to ask students questions like: *What do you think you might learn from this task? Who knows how to play this game?* This is a time for you to quickly explain the task while students listen.

2. **Read and discuss the Task Menu and Talking Points cards.** The Task Menus and Talking Points cards in workstations help students work independently. Students often struggle to remember all of the oral instructions they are given. Task Menus serve as a cheat sheet to help students recall what they are supposed to do. By referring directly to the Task Menu when introducing a task, you offer students both oral and written directions (both auditory and visual stimuli), so students are more likely to recall them. Also, by referring directly to the menus, you may clarify the written instructions at that time so students will better understand when they refer to them later.

   As with Step 1, this is a teacher-talk time. Students listen and learn while the teacher quickly delivers information.

3. **Model appropriate student behavior for the task.** With some tasks, modeling appropriate behavior might be simply modeling the playing of a math game. At other times, it will mean modeling the thinking and actions of mathematicians. When a problem is posed, how do mathematicians approach the task? Do they read and understand the problem first? Do they consider strategies that might be used to solve it? Do they gather materials? Model the kinds of behavior you want your students to exhibit at Math Workstations. Explicitly describe what you are doing. Be aware that students may not correctly infer expectations as you model behaviors. Explicitly share that you expect them to demonstrate these mathematical approaches to tasks as they work during Math Workshop.

   This step is also a time for attention to be focused on the teacher. Students observe and learn about the task.

4. **Ask students to role-play behavior appropriate for the task.** Have students act out what they would do as they work on the task. Ask the rest of the class to observe and assess the behavior. *What did these students do well? What improvements can they make?* You may notice aspects of behavior that students fail to see. If so, ask guiding questions that will lead students to recognize it themselves. For example, if a student uses an inefficient method to solve a problem, you might ask the student if there are any other strategies that would be more efficient. Be sure that the class hears any pertinent and helpful feedback, but do not allow this discussion to be too lengthy. The goal is to ensure that students understand the task and their responsibilities, but also to move as swiftly as possible into Math Workshop.

With this step, students assume an active role. The teacher facilitates this part of the introduction.

5. **Have students turn and talk about what the task is and how they will handle it. Address any questions that may arise during these talks.** Allow a minute or two for students to share. During this step, all students should be actively engaged as they share what they know about the task. Listen carefully to identify any misconceptions or confusion students have. If you note any problems with understanding the task, address them when you call students back together rather than with individual students. If one student has a misconception or is confused about something, others might as well. Give students an opportunity to ask any questions they may have regarding the task.

This final step requires students to communicate what they are thinking, reflect, and clarify any confusion or questions they may have. Teachers facilitate and provide additional information as needed.

Use your professional judgment when introducing workstation tasks to students. If the task is new to students and unlike anything they have done before, it will require a more detailed introduction. With tasks that are more familiar, the introduction may be abbreviated. A brief overview of these steps is shown in Figure 6.1.

Figure 6.1 Steps for Introducing Workstation Tasks

Steps	Instructional Method	Teacher/Student Roles
1. Share the purpose of the task.	teacher-centered	• Explain importance of task to student learning. • Discuss explicit links to math.
2. Examine and discuss the Student Task card and Talking Points card for the task.	teacher-centered	• Clarify instructions for task. • Reinforce mathematical vocabulary and math talk. • Demonstrate how to consult Student Task card and/or Talking Points card as a cheat sheet to remember what to do.
3. Model the appropriate student behavior for the task.	teacher-centered	• Demonstrate how students should engage with the task. • Share expectations for student behaviors.
4. Ask several students to role-play behavior appropriate for the task.	student-centered	• Students observe role-play of task by other students. • Students assess how well behaviors align with expectations. • Students provide feedback based on their assessment.
5. Have students turn and talk about the task and how they will handle it. Address any questions that may arise during these talks.	student-centered	• Students reflect on task and their responsibilities.

The Task Introduction Snapshots (pages 125–131) demonstrate how to introduce Math Workstation tasks and are designed for specific grade-level bands, but may be adapted for use with other grade levels.

Chapter 6

Task Introduction Snapshots

Addition Move One: Grade Levels K–2 (pages 99–101)

1. **Share the purpose of the task.**

   Teacher: *In Math Workshop today, you will work with a new task called* Addition Move One *to help you add numbers. It is important for mathematicians to be able to add fluently. This game helps us develop our mental math strategies as we find the sums of different addends. When we play the game, we have to think about which numbers we can add to win the game.*

2. **Read and discuss the Student Task card and Talking Points card.**

   Teacher: *Let's look at the Student Task card for the game.*

   Teacher displays the Student Task card on the board for students to see and refers to it directly during the discussion.

   The goal of the game is to get four spaces in a row on the game board. You will need the game board, two paper clips, and dry-erase markers. You may also use an Addition/Subtraction Chart if you need help adding the numbers.

   Teacher explains to students how to play the game.

   The first player puts two paper clips on the numbers at the bottom of the board. The numbers are the addends used to find the sum. Both paper clips may go on the same space. Find the sum, and mark that number on the board. Write your addition sentence in your math journal. Then, your partner takes a turn.

   Teacher reinforces mathematical vocabulary and math talk students will use while playing the game.

   It is important that you and your partner talk about the math you are doing. Look at the Talking Points card. Some of the words mathematicians might use are addend, sum, plus, add, addition, and double. Now, let's take a look at how we might describe mathematically what we are doing.

   Teacher reads the sentence starters from the Talking Points card.

3. **Model appropriate student behavior for the task.**

   Teacher: *I put both of my paper clips on the number 6. When I add 6 plus 6, my sum is 12. There are a lot of 12s on the board, but I think I will mark the 12 in row 5. I say to my partner, "I marked 12 on the board because 6 plus 6 equals 12. My addends were doubles this time." If I can't think of what to say, I may look at the Talking Points card to give me some ideas. Next, I am going to write "6 + 6 = 12" in my math journal.*

   Teacher thinks aloud to help students strategize their next move.

   As I get ready for my next turn, I think about how to get four spaces in a row. If I go across the row, I may find addends that will give me the sums 14, 17, or 5. Or, I might go up and down the column, so I look at the numbers above and below the 12 that I marked.

4. **Ask several students to role-play behavior appropriate for the task.**

   Teacher: *Lily and Victor, will you show us how you play this game? Please watch what they do so you may give them feedback.*

   Lily goes first. She places her paper clips on 5 and 8, and then marks 13 on the fifth row.

   Lily: *My addends are 5 and 8, which make 13.*

   Victor moves the paper clip from 8 to 3, and then marks the 8 in row 1.

   Victor: *8 is the sum of 5 and 3.*

   He writes *8 = 5 + 3* and *3 + 5 = 8* in his journal.

   Teacher: *Thank you, mathematicians, for showing us how to play the game. Okay, class. How about giving Lily and Victor some feedback. What do you think?*

   Student 1: *Lily, you talked about math, but you forgot to write in your journal.*

   Student 2: *Both of you used the math words for addition.*

   Student 3: *How did you decide which numbers to mark?*

   Student 4: *What addends will you choose next?*

   Student 5: *I like how Victor wrote the addition sentence two ways.*

   Teacher: *Thank you for the feedback. As we each work on this task, we want to think strategically, and remember to record our work.*

5. **Have students turn and talk about what the task is and how they will handle it. Address any questions that may arise during these talks.**

   Teacher: *Think about the task. Now, turn and tell a partner about how to play the game. What are some things you want to remember as you work on this task?*

   Teacher listens closely as students talk. From the talk, it seems that some students are more focused on the competition than on how the game will help them mathematically.

   Teacher: *I heard you share lots of good ideas about what you will be doing as you play this game. There is one thing I want to mention. In this game, there will be a winner. But, is that what is most important about this task? Please remember that games are fun, but we also need to think about the math. As we play the game, we are using strategies to find sums. This practice will help us become more fluent. Are there any questions about the game?*

   Student 6: *Can we move both paper clips when we take a turn?*

   Teacher: *Let's look back at the Student Task card. Reread step 3. "Player 2 moves one paper clip to a different addend…." Okay, mathematicians, let's begin Math Workshop.*

Task Introduction Snapshots

$1,000 House: Grade Levels 3–5 (pages 84–86)

1. **Share the purpose of the task.**

   Teacher: *In Math Workshop today, you will work with a new task called $1,000 House to help you better understand place value. Mathematicians developed the concept of place value to make writing the value of numbers easier and help them perform operations with multi-digit numbers. For this task, you will work with base-ten blocks that represent different values. You will see how they may be combined, or composed, in many different ways that all have the value of 1,000.*

2. **Read and discuss the Student Task card and Talking Points card.**

   Teacher: *Let's look at the Student Task card.*

   Teacher displays the Student Task card on the board for students to see and refers to it directly during the discussion.

   In this task, you really get to be creative. In fact, you will be architects designing a house. Your goal is to build a house worth exactly $1,000 using base-ten blocks. As you may see on the card, a flat is worth $100, a rod is worth $10, and a unit is worth $1. After you build your house, take a photo using the digital camera or draw a model in your math journal. Then, justify how the value of your design is $1,000 in at least two ways.

   Teacher reinforces mathematical vocabulary and math talk students will use while completing the task.

   As always, it is important that you and your partner talk about the math you are doing. Look at the Talking Points card. Some of the words mathematicians might use when working on this task are: place value, hundreds, tens, ones, sum, multiply, and product. The card also offers some suggestions for your math talk.

   Teacher reads the sentence starters from the Talking Points card.

3. **Model appropriate student behavior for the task.**

   Teacher: *If I were working on this task, I would think to myself: What do I know about 1,000 and how it compares to 100, 10, and 1. Then, I might visualize what a house made from base-ten blocks might look like. How large am I going to make it? Do I want to make the smallest house I can? Or, should I make the largest house possible? Maybe I should try to make it as realistic as possible.*

   Teacher helps students strategize by making a plan. Note that the teacher does not share the plan, only the thinking about how to begin. If teachers share a plan, most students copy it rather than doing their own thinking.

   Before mathematicians begin, they make a plan. Once I decide what I want to do, I get the base-ten blocks I need to build the house. As I build the house, I have to keep track of how many blocks I use and how much they are worth.

Teacher explains her procedure for completing the task.

I begin with these two flats. I know they are worth $100 and $100, so $200 altogether. Once I finish, I double check the blocks in my house are worth $1,000. Then, I take a picture and think of two different ways to justify my work. I might describe what I did in words, show my calculations of the values of the different blocks I used, or maybe come up with another way of sharing my thinking.

4. **Ask several students to role-play behavior appropriate for the task.**

   Teacher: *Kobi and Josh, will you show us how you would begin work on this task? While they work, please observe them carefully so you may give some feedback.*

   The two students immediately grab different blocks and put them together. They move them around to create a house shape and then pause.

   Alright, I see you have paused for a minute. Thank you for your work, Kobi and Josh. Let's think about their mathematical work so far.

   Student 1: *You got right to work and didn't waste any time.*

   Student 2: *How did you know what you were going to build? You didn't talk about it at all. Maybe it would help to make a plan first.*

   Student 3: *How did you figure out how much the blocks are worth that you put in the house?*

   Student 4: *You worked on building your house the whole time. You weren't distracted by anything else.*

   Teacher: *Thank you for giving your feedback from what you observed. Remember that mathematicians plan first so their work is more efficient. When I shared my thinking, I did it as though I was working alone. When you work with a partner, you have to not only plan in your head, but also talk with your partner about what you will do. Remember to use the Talking Points card if you need help to explain your thinking. You also noticed Kobi and Josh's good work habits. Keep these things in mind as you work on the task this week.*

5. **Have students turn and talk about what the task is and how to handle it. Address any questions that may arise during these talks.**

   Teacher: *Think for a minute about this task. After you think, turn and tell a partner about the $1,000 House task and what you will do as you work on this task. What are some things you want to remember to do?*

   Teacher listens closely as students talk. Many students mention planning ahead and sharing their ideas with their partners. Not many discussions mention the importance of having a way to calculate the value of the blocks in the house.

   I heard so many of you think like mathematicians as you talked about working on this task. You all recognize the need to have a plan before you begin and to try to visualize how the house might look. One of the really important parts of this task, though, is to make a plan for finding the value of the blocks you use and to be sure they equal $1,000. Are there any questions? Okay, mathematicians, let's begin Math Workshop.

Task Introduction Snapshots

Making Connections: Grade Levels 6-8 (pages 114-116)

1. Share the purpose of the task.

Teacher: *I am really excited about the new task you will work on in Math Workshop. Just like we use comprehension strategies to understand what we are reading, mathematicians use strategies to make connections in mathematics. Our understanding of mathematical concepts increases when we see how they are connected to other things. In Making Connections, you will reflect on some of the mathematical terms we are learning about this year and identify their connections to you, to other things you know about math, and to things in the real world.*

2. Read and discuss the Student Task card and Talking Points card.

Teacher: *Let's look at the Student Task card for the game.*

Teacher displays the Student Task card on the board and refers to it directly during the discussion.

Roll two number cubes and find the space on the vocabulary sheet where they intersect. You have a choice of two spaces—we'll talk about that in a minute. Then, you write that word in the Making Connections Graphic Organizer. *Now you start thinking! What connections can you make to that word? Record the connections in the appropriate space in the graphic organizer in "My Connections," "Math Connections," or "Real-World Connections." I can't wait to read some of the connections you make! You and a partner will work together on this to spark some mathematical ideas.*

Teacher reinforces mathematical vocabulary and math talk students will use while completing the task.

It is especially important that you and your partner talk about math as you work. Our Talking Points card is a bit different with this task because you are working with so many different mathematical vocabulary words. It includes the important word connection, *as well as some words that describe what you will do with this task: reflect, research, discuss, notice, and reason. I suggest you make use of our Math Word Wall and other vocabulary resources—including online resources—as you work. The card also offers some suggestions for your math talk. I think these will get you thinking.*

Teacher reads the sentence starters from the Talking Points card.

3. Model appropriate student behavior for the task.

Teacher: *I begin by rolling the number cubes. I rolled a 4 and a 2. When I look at the vocabulary sheet, I can go to row 4, column 2, and the word is percent. Or, I might go to row 2, column 4, where the word is absolute value. I will choose absolute value because it presents more of a challenge, and I like challenges. I write the words in the small section at the bottom of the graphic organizer labeled* Word.

Teacher explains personal connections to the word.

For the "My Connections" section, I have to think about what I know about the term and how it relates to me. I know value *means the worth of something, so I am going to add that to the graphic organizer. Absolute means total or completely. Let me add that. The term is also something that we learned when we practiced adding positive and negative integers. That's another connection to me.*

Teacher describes how the word connects to other math concepts.

For math connections, I may also make the connection to positive and negative integers. I can tell when I am adding them whether the sum will be positive or negative by comparing the absolute value of the addends. I will add that in "Math Connections."

Teacher makes real-world connections to the word.

"Real World Connections"—let me think about this. I don't often hear people talk about absolute values outside of math class. I think it could be important for figuring out total distances traveled. For example, I might walk two blocks away from my house and then one block back toward it. You might say I walked +2 blocks and then −1 block, so I am 1 block away from my house. But, to find out how far I walked, I want to consider the absolute values. So, I am going to put that down under "Real-World Connections."

Teacher encourages students to use available math resources to make additional math connections before they finish the task.

4. **Ask several students to role-play behavior appropriate for the task.**

   Teacher: *Lei and Carlos, please demonstrate for us how you would begin work on this task. Think aloud for us as you work. While they work, observe them carefully so you may give some feedback.*

   First Lei and Carlos must decide whether they will both roll two number cubes and then work on two separate words or whether they will each roll one number cube to determine a single word.

   Lei: *We can both roll two number cubes and work on two separate words.*

   Carlos: *Why don't we each roll one number cube and select a single word to work on together?*

   Lei: *I like your idea. Let's work together.*

   Lei rolls a 3 and Carlos rolls a 6. Together, they look at the vocabulary sheet. They have a choice between two words.

   Carlos: *Which word should we do, volume or polygon?*

   Lei: *Let's do polygon first, and if we have enough time we can choose a second word.*

   After a brief discussion about which word to use for the task, they settle on *polygon*. They begin by writing the word on the graphic organizer and then brainstorm their personal connections to the word.

Lei: *I remember learning about simple shapes when we were in kindergarten.*

Carlos: *My teacher had us sort shapes—some were polygons and some weren't.*

Next, they focus on math connections—the definition of polygon, which shapes are polygons and which are not, and how the term related to other math words such as line, side, or angle. When they consider connections to the real world, Lei and Carlos identify objects in their classroom that are polygons.

Carlos: *I see a lot of rectangles: this table, the window, the teacher's desk, this sheet of paper, the whiteboard.*

Lei: *The faces on this number cube are squares and so are the tiles on the floor.*

Carlos: *Oh, and look at the clock. It's in the shape of an octagon.*

Teacher: *Thank you for sharing your thinking with us. Let's reflect on what Lei and Carlos have done.*

Student 1: *You worked cooperatively and talked about polygons.*

Student 2: *You stayed focused and didn't talk about anything else.*

Student 3: *I wonder why you didn't use the Math Word Wall for ideas?*

Student 4: *When you talked about connections, you made me think about how I learned those things when I was in kindergarten.*

Student 5: *That word was easy. What would you do if you had a hard word to think about?*

Teacher: *Thank you for sharing your feedback with Lei and Carlos. It helps us all work more efficiently when we reflect on our performance. As you mentioned, they stayed on task and worked cooperatively. They did quite a bit of brainstorming, and when they use other resources that are available, I bet they may come up with even more ideas. Remember why this task is of value—good mathematicians make connections to help them understand math concepts and solve problems.*

5. **Have students turn and talk about what the task is and how to handle it. Address any questions that may arise during these talks.**

   Teacher: *Think for a minute about making connections and this task. Turn and talk with a partner. Share what you will do as you work on this activity.*

   The teacher listens closely as students talk.

   I am impressed by how many of you talked about the importance of making connections and about using the math resources you have. One thing some of you mentioned was the dilemma Lei and Carlos faced in deciding whether to each roll two number cubes and select two words or whether each of them would roll a number cube to select just one word. They made that decision on their own—I like how they took responsibility for doing that. As you work on this task, I will leave it up to you to decide how you will select the words. Do you have any questions? Okay, mathematicians, let's begin Math Workshop.

Assessing Student Readiness for Math Workshop

Students in most classrooms will be ready to begin Math Workshop after the first 15 days of practice, but not in all classrooms. Use your professional judgment to decide whether students are ready. Observe students as they work independently during Week 3, and consider these questions:

➡ Do students understand routines and procedures for Math Workshop?

➡ Do students engage in tasks without undue distraction?

➡ Are students able to solve problems they encounter without having to ask for assistance?

➡ Do students cooperate with others in their workstations?

➡ Do students communicate in soft voices within their groups about their work?

➡ Do students tend to their own work without distracting others?

Be realistic in your assessment of the overall ability of students to work independently. When students are given the responsibility of working on their own, it will rarely be perfect. Expect some issues to arise and do not be discouraged.

As you observe students' work habits, note any problems you see. Decide whether they are individual problems or are more systemic. When problems are specific to certain students, confer with those learners immediately to address your concerns. Discuss more generic issues with the entire class and provide additional opportunities to practice. While it is unwise to launch Math Workshop if excessive problems occur, it is also unwise to delay its implementation due to a smattering of issues that may be resolved with individual students. Figure 6.2 provides possible actions teachers may take when solving different types of behavior problems during Math Workshop.

Figure 6.2 Suggestions for Solving Behavior Problems during Math Workshop

Number of Students	Possible Actions
Just a few students	• Confer with those students about their behavior. Ask them to assess their behavior and identify how they may improve it. • Try to determine if the workstation tasks are at an appropriate level for the students. If not, adjust the task. • Create a nonverbal signal to let these students know when their behavior becomes inappropriate for workstations, so they may self-correct. • Have the students work beside you rather than in a workstation for a day or two.
Majority of students	• Call an end to Math Workshop for the day (no longer than a day or two). • Have students self-assess their behavior as a class to identify what they are doing well and in what areas they are having problems. • Tweak the established workshop routines and procedures, if needed, to address specific problem areas. • Re-examine the workstation tasks to ensure that they offer the appropriate level of challenge for students. • Revisit workshop routines and procedures with the entire class. • Provide additional time for students to practice the routines and procedures.

The First 15 Days

The following guide for the first 15 days of Guided Math Workshop offers suggested lessons to teach students the routines and procedures you want them to follow. Because the Guided Math Workshop model differs so greatly from the traditional whole-class instruction model, its implementation may be daunting for some teachers. They may be more comfortable easing their way into it. Partial implementation is also an approach that teachers often favor when introducing Math Workshop midyear.

If you choose to begin this way, remember that it is just as important to teach your students the workshop routines and procedures for a full 15 days as it is when beginning with full implementation. After all, it is hardly fair to students to significantly change their learning environment without first sharing your expectations and preparing them for the change. Attempting to begin Math Workshop without adequately preparing students is one of the most common causes of workshop problems. Even with preparation, bear in mind that Math Workshop may not run as smoothly because students will be spending less day-to-day time engaged in its practice.

Although an immediate full implementation may be a challenge, many teachers find that "diving in" rather than "tiptoeing in" is the most efficient way to approach Math Workshop.

Week 1 – Establishing Routines and Procedures for Math Workshop

During the first week of Guided Math Workshop, the instructional focus is on helping students discover what Math Workshop is and why it is important to their learning. Help students understand that Math Workshop is a time when they work independently on math to become better mathematicians. During this time, focus on teaching students basic routines and procedures. Encourage them to see themselves as mathematicians. Through whole-class discussions, the creation of anchor charts, and the modeling of correct and incorrect behaviors, students learn how important Math Workshop is in offering them "just right" mathematics and begin to recognize their own roles in making learning a success. Students learn that the term *just right* means "math that targets their immediate instructional needs." This may involve bridging the gaps in their background knowledge and skills, providing an intervention for current learning topics, or offering additional challenges. Most students really appreciate the move away from one-size-fits-all instruction.

When teaching students Math Workshop routines and procedures, offer experiences that include input from all three memory systems: visual, auditory, and kinesthetic. Research shows that when information is stored in more than one of these systems, memory is improved (Grinder 1995; Boushey and Moser 2006).

As shown in Figure 6.3, instruction for the first week includes input from all three memory systems. Whole-class discussions provide auditory reinforcement of the ideas being emphasized, anchor charts with recorded information from class discussions serve as visual cues, and the modeling and practice of routines and procedures offer kinesthetic learning experiences.

Figure 6.3 The Memory System in the First Week

Memory System	Routines and Procedures
auditory	class discussions
visual	anchor charts
kinesthetic	modeling and practice

Although teaching and learning strategies used in the classroom are often employed without students being aware of their use, it is beneficial for students to understand what Math Workshop is and why it is being implemented. Many students are already acutely aware of the limitations of whole-class instruction. Some students are bored by lessons that focus on areas of math that they have already mastered. Some students with significant gaps in background knowledge and skills feel lost during lessons that require previous knowledge. Other students may be shy or reluctant to share ideas with the entire class. During the first week, follow the plan shown in Figure 6.4 to establish routines and procedures for Math Workshop.

Figure 6.4 Week 1—Establishing Routines and Procedures for Math Workshop

Day 1	
Focus	What is Math Workshop?
Learning Outcomes	Students describe what Math Workshop is and why it is important.
Activities	Class discussion and creation of an anchor chart identifying what Math Workshop is and ideas about why it is important.
Teacher Notes	Math Workshop helps students • develop better understanding and fluency in math. • learn to work independently. • learn to work with partners. • work in small groups and confer one-on-one with the teacher.

Day 2	
Focus	What does Math Workshop look like and sound like?
Learning Outcomes	Students identify how Math Workshop should look and sound.
Activities	Review and further clarify what Math Workshop is and why it is important. Discuss what successful Math Workshop should look like and sound like. Add to the anchor chart about Math Workshop.
Teacher Notes	Math Workshop looks like • students working as mathematicians. • students using manipulatives. • students writing about math. • students playing math games. Math Workshop sounds like • students talking about math. • students talking at appropriate volumes.

Day 3	
Focus	What do good mathematicians do as they work during Math Workshop?
Learning Outcomes	Students know the routines and procedures for Math Workshop.
Activities	Review and further clarify the Math Workshop anchor chart. Discuss expectations for student behavior during Math Workshop. Create an anchor chart of no more than five or six criteria for routines and procedures. Explain to students that it is expected they follow routines and procedures, but that problems may arise. Discuss possible problems students might encounter and how to solve them independently.
Teacher Notes	Examples for routines and procedures include • staying on task and in your workspace. • cleaning up your workspace when you finish. • speaking in a soft voice about your math work. • asking if you do not know what to do. • using math materials appropriately.

Day 4	
Focus	What do good mathematicians do as they work during Math Workshop?
Learning Outcomes	Students know routines and procedures for independent work during Math Workshop.
Activities	Review and further clarify what Math Workshop is and why it is important. Revisit the anchor chart on routines and procedures. Focus on the first two or three routines. Examine each routine in more detail.
Teacher Notes	For each routine • model how it looks and does not look. • have students role-play examples. • have students role-play non-examples. • have students role-play to show the correct behavior.
Day 5	
Focus	What do good mathematicians do as they work during Math Workshop?
Learning Outcomes	Students know routines and procedures for their independent work during Math Workshop.
Activities	Review what Math Workshop is and why it is important. Revisit the anchor chart of routines and procedures. Focus on the remaining routines. Examine each routine in more detail.
Teacher Notes	For each routine • model how it looks and does not look. • have students role-play examples. • have students role-play non-examples. • have students role-play to show the correct behavior.

The sample lessons on pages 138–144 (for the first week of Math Workshop) are designed for specific grade-level bands, but may be adapted for use with other grade levels.

What Does Math Workshop Look Like and Sound Like?

Overview

Students discuss the roles of teacher and students during Math Workshop and define what Math Workshop should look like and sound like so all students can grow as mathematicians. Students contribute ideas to a class anchor chart that is posted for future reference.

Objective

Know how Math Workshop should look and sound.

Materials

• chart paper
• markers

Procedure

1. Remind students what Math Workshop is and why it is important (*students working independently on math to become better mathematicians*). Create an anchor chart by writing a statement about the purpose and importance of Math Workshop (see Figure 6.5 for examples).

2. Divide the anchor chart into four sections, and label two sections *Your Job* and *The Teacher's Job*. You might also want to personalize the teacher section with your name. Explain that during Math Workshop the teacher and students have different, but equally important, jobs. Have students share what they think their jobs should be. Record student responses in the section labeled *Your Job*. If not mentioned, lead students to include *work independently* and *practice math*.

3. Tell students the teacher has two primary jobs during Math Workshop. Those jobs are to teach students in small groups and to confer with students about their mathematical thinking. Ask students to offer additional suggestions about the teacher's job. Record ideas in the section labeled *The Teacher's Job*. Remind students your job depends on them doing theirs—working independently.

4. Label the two remaining sections on the anchor chart *Looks Like* and *Sounds Like*. Tell students that when they are working independently during Math Workshop, it should look and sound a certain way. Ask students to think about a visitor coming into their classroom. What might the visitor see that would indicate mathematicians are hard at work? Lead students to describe not only what students are doing (e.g., completing math tasks, talking and writing about math, playing math games), but also what they are using (e.g., math tools and manipulatives). Record their responses on the anchor chart.

5. Discuss what the room should sound like during Math Workshop. Decide on an appropriate voice level for math discussions. Stress that students should be respectful of the work other mathematicians are doing around them at all times.

6. Post the completed anchor chart in a highly visible location in the room. Refer to it frequently while setting the stage for Math Workshop and occasionally throughout the year if students need a refresher.

Chapter 6

Figure 6.5 Sample Math Workshop Anchor Charts

Your Job
- Work independently
- Work with partners
- Follow directions
- Engage in math tasks
- Listen and learn

The Teacher's Job
- Help mathematicians
- Confer with mathematicians
- Listen and learn from you!

Math Workshop Is...
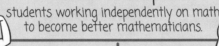
students working independently on math to become better mathematicians.

Looks Like...
- Students working on math
- Students using math tools and manipulatives
- Students playing math games
- Students staying in one place

Sounds Like...
- Quiet conversations about math
- Students taking care not to disturb others

People working on math
Writing in math journal
Have fun in math stations
Helping friends
Solve problems
Teamwork

Math talks
Quiet level 1 talks

Math Workshop

Your Job 😊😊
Work in math stations
Listening and learning
Follow directions
Pay attention
Practice math

Ms. Tran's Job
Help mathematicians
Work with mathematicians
Teach math
Listen and learn from YOU

Math Workshop Routines and Procedures

Overview

The teacher leads the students in a class discussion on routines and procedures for Math Workshop so all students can grow as mathematicians. Students contribute ideas to a class anchor chart that is posted for future reference.

Objective

Demonstrate understanding of routines and procedures for independent work during Math Workshop.

Materials

- *Math Workshop Routines and Procedures* activity sheet (page 141)
- chart paper
- markers

Procedure

1. Prior to the lesson, develop a list of five to six routines and procedures you want in place for Math Workshop. Create a true/false activity sheet with statements related to your desired procedures, or use the activity sheet shown on page 141.

2. Remind students that Math Workshop is a time to work independently and practice math. Remind them that while they work independently, you will meet with students for small-group instruction or math conferences. So, it is important to have routines and procedures in place to ensure that Math Workshop operates effectively.

3. Tell students they will work in groups to complete the *Math Workshop Routines and Procedures* activity sheet. Reminds students to reference the anchor chart created in the Day 2 lesson that describes how Math Workshop should look and sound when responding to the statements on the activity sheet. Distribute a copy of the activity sheet to each group, and give students time to complete it.

4. Ask groups to share their responses for each statement. Create an anchor chart listing the Math Workshop routines and procedures necessary to have Math Workshop look and sound as it should.

Name: _____ Date: _____

Math Workshop Routines and Procedures

Directions: Decide whether each statement is true or false. If it is false, rewrite it as a true statement.

1. Move to a new workspace as often as you like during Math Workshop.

   _____

2. Interrupt the teacher to ask for directions.

   _____

3. Math materials are unbreakable. They are easily replaced.

   _____

4. Speak loudly to your partner so everyone in the room can hear you.

   _____

5. Sharpen pencils, take restroom breaks, and talk about the lunch menu during Math Workshop.

   _____

6. Leave workstation materials out for others to clean up when you are finished.

   _____

7. My behavior does not affect anyone else during Math Workshop.

   _____

Week 1: Grades 6-8
Sample Lesson for Day 4 or 5 in the First 15 Days Plan

Math Workshop Routines and Procedures

Overview

Students act out and critique examples and nonexamples of Math Workshop routines and procedures.

Objective

Know the routines and procedures for Math Workshop.

Materials

- anchor chart created on Day 2
- *Routines and Procedures* cards (page 143)

Procedure

Note: To emphasize the importance of routines and procedures and to allow students ample opportunity to practice, this lesson should be taught over two days. Concentrate on two to three procedures each day.

1. Prior to this lesson, copy and cut out the cards on page 143, or use the blank cards on page 144 with your own Math Workshop routines and procedures.

2. Revisit the anchor chart created on Day 2. Remind students that during Math Workshop you will be working with students in small groups, so they must work independently at their work spaces.

3. Tell students that over the next two days, they will role-play to show how Math Workshop should and should not look. Divide the class into groups of 2–3 students. Distribute a card to each group of students. Explain that each card lists a routine or procedure and a picture of either a tomato or clapping hands. Explain that throwing rotten tomatoes is often associated with a poor theatrical performance. If they receive a card with clapping hands, they will role-play how the procedure should look. If their card shows a tomato, they will role-play how the procedure should not look.

4. Allow time for students to practice their performances. Then, choose a group of students to role-play the procedure from their card. Ask the rest of the class—the audience— to either clap their hands or mimic throwing tomatoes to indicate if they think the performance showed how the procedure should or should not look. Have the class critique the performance. Continue over two days until students have acted out all routines and procedures.

Routines and Procedures

 Stay on task and at your workspace.

 Stay on task and at your workspace.

 Clean up your workspace when you finish.

Clean up your workspace when you finish.

 Speak in a soft voice about your task.

 Speak in a soft voice about your task.

 Work on tasks independently.

 Work on tasks independently.

 Use materials appropriately.

 Use materials appropriately.

Routines and Procedures *(cont.)*

Week 2 – Math Workstations: The Nuts and Bolts of Math Workshop

Once students learn what Math Workshop is, why it is important, and how it should look and sound, they should be introduced to Math Workstations. During Week 2 (see Figure 6.6), focus on instruction in the following areas:

➡ Review routines and procedures taught in Week 1, but also familiarize students with behavior expectations when working at math workspaces.

➡ Identify designated workspaces of the classroom.

➡ Explain what Math Workstation tasks are and how to use them.

➡ Assign a simple Math Workstation task (see page 71 for suggested tasks) so students may practice routines and procedures.

➡ Explain how to use Task Menus (see pages 44–45) and Student Task cards (see page 45).

➡ Demonstrate how to use Talking Points cards (see page 46).

➡ Emphasize student responsibilities at workspaces.

➡ Demonstrate how to clean up workspaces and materials.

Students should have opportunities to practice working on Math Workstation tasks. Continue to help students build stamina by gradually increasing the amount of time they work independently. Give specific feedback about what students are doing well. Do not hesitate to stop a practice session if students are not following routines and procedures. It is better to stop, review, and try again. This is the time when behavioral issues should be resolved, so Math Workshop will run smoothly later in the school year.

Figure 6.6 Week 2—Establishing Routines and Procedures for Math Workstations

Day 6	
Focus	Where do we work during Math Workshop?
Learning Outcomes	Students know where they may work during Math Workshop.
Activities	Review routines and procedures. Show students where they will work and how to transition to those workspaces. Have students practice moving to their workspaces while following routines and procedures. Then, have students self-assess. What did they do well? What needs more work? Repeat the process as needed.
Teacher Notes	To model the process, have students • move to their assigned workspaces. • return to their seats. • debrief and self-assess how they did.

Day 7	
Focus	What are Math Workstations? Where are they stored?
Learning Outcomes	Students know where Math Workstations are stored and how they access them and put them away.
Activities	Review routines and procedures and where students work. Introduce where Math Workstations are stored and how students access them. Discuss how students should clean up workspaces and return Math Workstations. Provide enough Math Workstations for students to work in small groups or pairs. Each station should have the same simple task. Have students practice getting Math Workstations, moving to workspaces, and putting them away. Then, students self-assess how they did. Repeat as needed.
Teacher Notes	To model the process • assign groups of 4–5 students. • give each group a Math Workstation. • ask students to debrief and self-assess how they did.

Day 8	
Focus	How will we know what to do with a Math Workstation?
Learning Outcomes	Students use Task Menus and Student Task cards.
Activities	Review routines and procedures. Show students what they may expect to find when they open their Math Workstation. Focus on Task Menus or Student Task cards. Model how students will find the Task Menu and Student Task cards in the Math Workstation and use them to choose and complete tasks. Using Math Workstations from Day 7, ask students to get the workstation, find the Task Menu and Student Task cards. Then, debrief.
Teacher Notes	To model the process • assign groups of 4–5 students. • give each group a Math Workstation. • have each group find the Task Menu. • have each group find the Student Task cards. • ask students to debrief and self-assess how they did.

Day 9	
Focus	What are Talking Points cards?
Learning Outcomes	Students use Talking Points cards to engage in mathematical talk.
Activities	Review routines and procedures. Show students what they will find in a Math Workstation. Focus on Talking Points cards. Model how to use Talking Points cards to talk about math tasks. Ask students to role-play using cards and model incorrect usages. Have students share feedback and then role-play the correct usages. Ask students to get their Math Workstation and move to their workspaces. Remind them to practice using Talking Points cards. Then, debrief.
Teacher Notes	To model the process • assign groups of 4–5 students. • give each group a Talking Points card. • allow time for students to practice. • ask students to debrief and self-assess how they did.
Day 10	
Focus	How do we use Math Workstations independently?
Learning Outcomes	Students get Math Workstations, move to their workspaces, find Task Menus and Student Task cards, complete tasks, use Talking Points cards, and return Math Workstations.
Activities	Review and model the process of getting Math Workstations: using Task Menu and Student Task cards, using Talking Points cards, completing Student Task cards, and then returning the Workstation when asked. Introduce a signal for completing tasks and cleaning up workspaces. Have students practice the entire process, debrief, and then repeat. Refer to the anchor chart if needed.
Teacher Notes	To model the process • show students a Task Menu and explain workstation options. • show students a Student Task card and model how to read the directions. • ask students to share what they observed. • have students role-play a Student Task card and solicit feedback from the class. • ask students to debrief and self-assess how they did.

Sample lessons on pages 148–152 (for the second week of Math Workshop) are designed for specific grade-level bands, but may be adapted for use with other grade levels.

Chapter 6

Getting Math Workstations and Putting Them Away

Overview

Students learn where Math Workstations are stored, how to access them, and procedures for cleaning and putting them away by watching the teacher model the process, by role-playing the process with a partner, and by practicing independently.

Objective

Learn where Math Workstations are stored, how to access them, and how to put them away.

Materials

- Math Workstation of your choosing

Procedure

1. Review spaces in the classroom where students will work during Math Workshop and routines and procedures for transitions. Call on students to role-play what it looks like to move carefully and purposefully around the room. Ask students to describe behaviors they observed during role-play.

2. Introduce the management system you will use for Math Workshop (pages 23–26). Tell students they will use the management system to determine which Math Workstation they will be working on.

3. Show students where Math Workstations are stored and where they may find additional materials they may need during Math Workshop (e.g., paper, writing tools, manipulatives). Explain how containers are labeled and how students may identify the container they are looking for. Make connections between the labeling of containers and the management system.

4. While students observe, model how to determine the correct Math Workstation using the management system, retrieve the workstation from the storage location, and move to the designated workspace. Give the signal to clean up, and model how to return the Math Workstation to the storage area. Ask students to share what they observed.

5. Choose two students to role-play how to retrieve a Math Workstation, take it to the workspace, and put it back. Ask the other students to critique what they did well and how they could improve.

6. Have students practice the entire process—using the management system to determine the correct task, retrieving the task, moving to the appropriate workspace, and putting the Math Workstation away. Debrief the process and repeat.

Chapter 6

Using Task Menus and Student Task Cards

Overview

Students learn how to use the Task Menu and Student Task cards to successfully perform a Math Workstation task independently.

Objective

Demonstrate how to use Task Menus and Student Task cards.

Materials

- Task Menu
- Math Workstation task of your choosing
- Student Task card of your choosing

Procedure

1. Review routines and procedures for accessing Math Workstation tasks, moving to designated workspaces, and putting tasks away.

2. Remind students that during Math Workshop you will either be working with small groups of students or conferring with individual students, and it is their responsibility to work independently, solve their own problems, and make the best use of their time. Explain that each Math Workstation will contain a Task Menu and Student Task cards that will help them be independent learners. Display samples similar to those shown in Figure 6.7 and Figure 6.8.

3. Show students the Task Menu from a practice Math Workstation. Explain that the menu gives the workstation options, and the Student Task card gives all the information needed to perform each task on the menu. Model the correct way to read the directions on the Student Task card, stopping to think aloud as you process each step. Tell students how important it is to understand one step before moving on to the next. Ask students to share what they observed as you modeled the process. Continue by modeling how not to use the Student Task card (e.g., trying to perform the task without reading the instructions). Ask students to compare the two processes.

4. Ask two students to role-play reading a Student Task card while the class observes. Solicit feedback from the class by asking: *Did the students read and carefully consider each step of the instructions? Did they discuss and resolve any instructions they were unsure of or problems they encountered?*

Chapter 6

5. Remind students that the Task Menu and Student Task cards will help them work independently and successfully perform each task. Have students get their Math Workstation task, move to their designated workpace, and use the Student Task card to perform the task. Carefully observe students while they work, making note of their use of the proper routines and procedures.

6. After students have had time to practice the task, give the signal for students to clean up their workspaces and return their Math Workstation task to the proper location. Have students debrief and reflect on how well they followed the routines and procedures, what they did well, and what still needs work.

Figure 6.7 Sample GUIDE Workstation Task Menu (Grades 3–5)

GUIDE Task Menu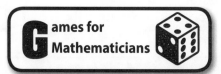

Must Do	
Math Workstation task	**"Just right" task**
• Area and Perimeter War • 3-D Dimensional Figure Memory	✓
May Do	
Math Workstation task	**"Just right" task**
• Difference from 5,000	✓
• Vocabulary Bingo	
• Place Value I Have/Who Has	✓

Figure 6.8 Sample Student Workstation Task Card (Grades 3–5)

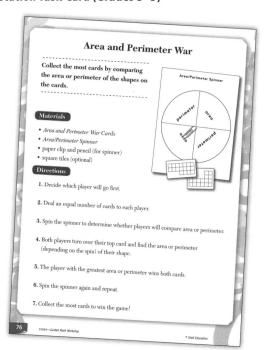

Week 2: Grades 6–8
Sample Lesson for Day 9 in the First 15 Days Plan

Math Talking Points Cards

Overview

Students learn how to use the Talking Points cards that are included in each Math Workstation task.

Objective

Understand that a Talking Points card provides math vocabulary and sentence stems that will help them engage in mathematical conversations.

Materials

- Math Workstation task of your choosing
- Talking Points card of your choosing

Procedure

1. Begin the lesson by asking students to turn and talk with a partner about what they know about Math Workstation tasks. Ask students to share some of their ideas with the whole class. Students should be able to describe where Math Workstations are stored, how to access them, how to use the Task Menu, and how to put them away. If necessary, reteach procedures that students did not discuss to reinforce understanding.

2. Introduce Talking Points cards by telling students that when working with mathematics, precision is important. Mathematicians use precise mathematical vocabulary to explain and justify their mathematical thinking precisely. Talking Points cards help students as they practice this important skill.

3. Use one of the practice Math Workstation tasks to show students a Talking Points card similar to Figure 6.9. Explain that it will always include the important vocabulary words related to the task and may include visual representations or sentence stems to support mathematical discourse.

4. Model the use of Talking Points cards, explicitly linking your math talk to what is on the card. Ask students to share what they observed. Next, model math talk that does not include mathematical vocabulary words and lacks precision. Again, ask students to share what they observed. Ask them: *How were the two math talks different? Which was more precise? Why?*

5. Ask two students to role-play using the Talking Points card as the class watches and then critiques the math talk. Ask students: *What did you notice about the math talk? How did the students use the Talking Points card? Are there any other ways they could have used it that would have made their conversation more precise?*

6. Ask students to get their Math Workstation tasks and move to their workspaces to practice the procedures they have learned. Monitor their use of routines and procedures that have been taught.

7. After sufficient practice time, have students clean their workspace, put away their workstations, and then debrief. Ask students to reflect. What did they do well, individually, or as a class? What do they need to work on?

Figure 6.9 Sample Talking Points Card (Grades 6–8)

Talking Points

Vocabulary	Talk like a mathematician:
• base number • exponent • power • scientific notation • standard form	Scientific notation is helpful when working with very small or very large numbers because _____. I can convert a number from standard form to scientific notation by _____. I can change a number written in standard form to scientific notation by _____. A negative exponent means that _____.

Week 3 – Thinking Like Mathematicians: Focusing on Mathematical Practices

During Week 3 of the first 15 days (see Figure 6.10), give students increased time to practice routines and procedures and build their stamina for working independently. Because Math Workshop routines and procedures should already be familiar to students, your lessons for this week may center on helping students think like mathematicians. Target suggested mathematical process skills during the first four days of the week (e.g., Communication and Representation, Connections, Reasoning and Proof, Problem Solving). On Friday, review what has been learned and practiced, and then focus on the critical issue of student accountability.

Fifteen days are included in this plan for teaching routines and procedures students must know and follow for implementing an effective Math Workshop. In some classrooms, students may need more or less time. As a teaching professional, decide when your class is ready to work independently while you teach small groups of students or confer with individual students. Trust your instincts, but do not be anxious about taking this first step forward with your class.

If you begin Math Workshop and find that students are not quite ready, simply call a halt to it. Regroup and reflect on what went wrong. Try to identify where problems arose. You may choose to discuss them with your students to find out what their perceptions are of the problem. Ask yourself these questions:

➡ *Is there a particular place in the classroom where the problems arise?* If so, you may need to rearrange the workspaces or introduce a procedure that will solve the problem.

➡ *Is there a specific time when the problems tend to occur?* Consider what is happening at that time and what you can do to eliminate the source of the problem?

➡ *Is there a problem with the routines or procedures? Are there aspects of workshop management that you did not consider?* If so, you may need to modify or add to the routines and procedures.

➡ *Are the problems caused by students who did not understand the behavioral expectations you set?* If so, try to locate exactly where and when the problems arose. Reteach routines and behaviors to ensure students *know* how they are expected to behave.

➡ *Do problems arise because students understand the routines and procedures, but fail to follow them?* Consider whether students need more practice time to build stamina. You may decide to provide additional practice time or to shorten your Math Workshop initially, until the stamina of your students increases.

Often, just the fact that Math Workshop abruptly ends if students are not meeting behavioral expectations is sufficient motivation for students to improve behavior. Students enjoy working independently and in small-group settings. When they discover Math Workshop ends when they fail to follow established routines and procedures, most students are highly motivated to improve their behavior.

Sometimes an individual student may require extra support to develop the capacity to work independently. If an individual's behavior consistently interrupts Math Workshop, provide targeted support for that student rather than ending Math Workshop for the entire class. You may choose to do something as simple as having the student work independently at a desk beside you if disruptions continue to occur.

Figure 6.10 Week 3—Thinking Like Mathematicians: Focusing on Mathematical Practices

Day 11	
Focus	How do mathematicians communicate and represent their mathematical thinking?
Learning Outcomes	Students understand that mathematicians share their thinking by talking about it, writing about it, and representing it in multiple ways. Students understand they are expected to write about and represent their mathematical thinking daily.
Activities	Pose a simple problem to be solved together by the class. After a solution is found, model how to talk about the mathematics involved in finding the solution. As a shared writing task in which the teacher is the scribe, describe the problem-solving process. Emphasize the importance of staying focused and using appropriate mathematical vocabulary. Discuss the use of the Math Word Wall. Introduce a Math Workstation task that requires students to solve a problem and then write about how it was solved. Have students practice the entire Math Workshop process. During this practice time, do not allow students to interact with you. Observe and end the workshop practice if students are having difficulty following the routines and procedures. Debrief after their workshop practice. Refer back to the anchor chart for routines and procedures, if needed.
Teacher Notes	To model the process • solve a problem with the class and engage in shared writing to describe the process. • have students discuss how to communicate clearly the problem-solving process they used. • assign a workstation task in which students solve a simple problem. • have students reflect on and self-assess their performance following routines and procedures as they build stamina.

Day 12	
Focus	How do mathematicians make mathematical connections?
Learning Outcomes	Students understand that mathematicians expand their thinking by exploring how math concepts connect to other areas of math, to their own experiences, and to the real world.
Activities	Introduce the idea of making connections by linking it to literacy comprehension strategies. Choose a math word or concept and think aloud, sharing how you think it connects with other math concepts, things in your own life, and the real world. Choose another math word or concept for the class to consider. Create an anchor chart recording students' connections to the word or concept. Introduce a Math Workstation task that requires students to make connections to a math word or concept. Have students practice the entire Math Workshop process, debrief, and then practice again with another debrief session. Refer back to the anchor chart for routines and procedures, if needed.
Teacher Notes	To model the process • create an anchor chart to record mathematical connections. • model a math-to-self connection by sharing a personal story and adding it to the chart. • model a math-to-world connection by sharing a current event topic and adding it to the chart. • model several math-to-math connections by showing how math concepts are related and adding them to the chart. • assign a task that requires students to make connections. • have students reflect on their performance following routines and procedures as they build stamina.

Day 13	
Focus	How do mathematicians reason and justify their thinking?
Learning Outcomes	Students understand that mathematicians justify their mathematical thinking.
Activities	Ask students why teachers ask them "How do you know?" Discuss how it is important to not only be able to state a mathematical fact, but also to justify it. Brainstorm synonymous words and phrases for the word *justify* (e.g., explain, prove, express, give reasons why, illustrate why, describe). Provide examples of mathematical work—some of which include justification and some of which do not. Have students examine the examples and discuss whether each example includes justification. Introduce a Math Workstation task that requires students to justify their work. Practice the entire Math Workshop process. With each session, give more time to build stamina. Do not allow students to interact with you during these practice sessions. Observe and end the practice if students are having difficulty following routines and procedures. Discuss any problems that arise on the debrief by students.

Teacher Notes	To model the process • share examples that clearly demonstrate students' mathematical thinking. • share examples in which students do not justify their thinking. • have students examine the samples to determine which include strong justification and which do not. • provide a workstation task requiring students to justify their mathematical thinking. • have students reflect on their performance following routines and procedures as they build stamina.

Day 14

Focus	What process do mathematicians use when problem solving?
Learning Outcomes	Students understand the most efficient and effective way to solve mathematical problems is following a logical process.
Activities	Introduce the problem-solving process by sharing a personal scenario of a problem to be solved. Describe being unsure where to begin or what needs to be done to solve it. Share the problem-solving graphic organizer. Discuss each step in the problem-solving process. As a class, solve a sample problem using the graphic organizer. Introduce a Math Workstation task with a simple problem for which students will use the problem-solving graphic organizer. Practice the entire Math Workshop process. With each practice session, give students more time to build stamina. During these practice times, do not allow students to interact with the teacher. Observe and end the practice if students are having difficulty following the routines and procedures. Discuss any problems that arise in the debrief as students self-assess their work as a class.
Teacher Notes	To model the process • solve a problem together as a class using a graphic organizer. • assign a workstation task requiring problem solving to practice independent work and build stamina. • have students reflect on and self-assess their performance following routines and procedures as they build stamina.

Chapter 6

Day 15	
Focus	How are mathematicians accountable for their work?
Learning Outcomes	Students understand they are accountable for the work they do in Math Workshop, in the same way mathematicians take responsibility for their work.
Activities	Review with students the Math Workshop anchor chart, as well as the Routines and Procedures anchor chart. Give examples of how mathematicians are accountable for their work. Tell students, "Accountants are people who rely on their computations. Engineers build bridges that must hold the weight of cars and trucks. Parents budget their incomes." Remind students they are also accountable for their independent work. Share examples of ways they will be held accountable (e.g., recording sheets or math journals). This lesson should be brief so that most of the class period is spent practicing how to work independently. Introduce Math Workstation tasks with forms of accountability. Practice the entire Math Workshop process. Include a debrief and self-assessment by students to address any remaining problems.
Teacher Notes	To model the process • provide examples of how mathematicians are held accountable for their work. • show students a recording sheet and a math journal they will use during Math Workshop. • practice the process with a Math Workstation task. • have students reflect on and self-assess their performance following routines and procedures when working independently.

The sample lessons on pages 157–162 (for the third week of Math Workshop) are designed for specific grade-level bands, but may be adapted for use with other grade levels.

Mathematicians Share Their Thinking

Overview

In the context of problem solving, the teacher models how mathematicians communicate their thinking by talking, writing, and using multiple representations. Students solve a problem using linking cubes and their examples are recorded on an anchor chart.

Objective

Understand that mathematicians share their thinking by talking about it, writing about it, and representing it in multiple ways.

Materials

- chart paper
- markers
- linking cubes

Procedure

1. Prior to the lesson, create an anchor chart with the following problem: *Four students want to play a math game. Each student needs three game pieces. How many game pieces will the students need in all?*

2. Tell students that mathematicians often work together to solve problems, and today they will help you solve a problem. Display the anchor chart, and read the problem aloud.

3. Remind students that mathematicians often use tools when solving problems. Have students turn and talk to a partner about a strategy they might use to solve the problem with linking cubes.

4. Explain to students that it is important for mathematicians to communicate their thinking by talking, and they will share their solutions in class often. Call on several pairs of students to share their strategies for solving the problem. Model each strategy. Encourage students to discuss whether they agree or disagree with the solutions, and explain that it is okay to disagree with another mathematician's thinking.

5. After successfully solving the problem as a class, tell students you will record their thinking on the anchor chart. Show multiple ways of representing the problem, labeling each representation. Some examples are shown in Figure 6.11. Post the anchor chart for future reference.

Chapter 6

Figure 6.11 Sample Mathematical Thinking Anchor Chart

How Mathematicians Represent Their Thinking

Problem: Four students want to play a math game. Each student needs three game pieces. How many game pieces will the students need in all?

Write a solution statement.
The students need 12 playing pieces.

Draw a Diagram.

1 4 7 10
2 5 8 11
3 6 9 12

Make a Table.

Players	Playing Pieces
1	3
2	6
3	9
4	12

Write an Equation.

$3 + 3 + 3 + 3 = 12$

Use Tally Marks.

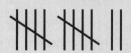

Use a Number Line.

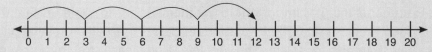

Chapter 6

Mathematicians Make Connections

Overview

Students make math-to-self, math-to-world, and math-to-math connections to a concept or word.

Objective

Understand that mathematicians expand their thinking by exploring how math concepts connect to other areas of math, to their own experiences, and to the real world.

Materials

- chart paper
- markers
- newspaper articles for math-to-world connections

Procedure

1. Prior to the lesson, divide the chart paper into three sections and label them *Math-to-Self*, *Math-to-World*, and *Math-to-Math* (see Figure 6.12). Choose a mathematical concept and add it to the anchor chart as a title. Plan out your connections to the mathematical concept or word ahead of time so you may effectively model the process of making connections for students.

2. Ask students to describe how making connections when reading (text-to-text, text-to-self, and text-to-world) helps them better understand the text. Explain that we make connections in mathematics as well. As we learn new mathematical concepts, our connections to known ideas help us make sense of new learning. Understanding ways in which mathematics is used in the world around us gives purpose to our learning.

3. Explicitly model several math-to-self connections, adding them to the chart. Explain to students that math-to-self connections are ways the concept is connected to their personal experiences. For example, *I enjoy cooking, so when I think of fractions I think of measuring the ingredients listed in a recipe. If I'm not careful reading the fractions and measuring accurately, my dish won't taste good and no one will eat it!* Invite students to share their own math-to-self connections, and add them to the chart.

4. Explain to students that making math-to-world connections helps them understand the role mathematics plays in the world around them. Discuss how current event topics relate to the math they are learning to expand their awareness of local, national, and world events. Share news articles, and explain the connection to the concept the class is discussing. Add the connections to the anchor chart.

5. Explain to students that making math-to-math connections helps them construct new learning from previously learned concepts and highlight the interconnectivity of mathematical ideas. It is through these connections that students come to deeply understand and appreciate mathematics. Have several math-to-math connections ready to discuss and add to the chart.

Figure 6.12 Sample Mathematical Connections Anchor Chart (Grades 3–5)

Making Mathematical Connections with Fractions

Math-to-Self	Math-to-World	Math-to-Math
• sharing a pizza • measuring ingredients when cooking • distance from home to school is $\frac{3}{4}$ mile • fuel gauge in my parent's car • half-off sale items	• $\frac{2}{3}$ of members in Congress voted "yes" on a bill • Fraction of people in a study who responded positively to a new treatment • Percentage of energy costs saved by using natural gas	• division—equal groups • geometry—using 6 triangles to make a hexagon (pattern blocks) • clock—15 minutes is $\frac{1}{4}$ of an hour • ruler made up of fractional parts • related to percents and decimals

Mathematicians Solve Problems

Overview

The teacher shares a personal scenario of a problem, models the use of a problem-solving graphic organizer, and guides students through each step of the problem-solving process.

Objective

Understand the most efficient and effective way to solve mathematical problems is following a logical process.

Materials

- chart paper
- markers

Procedure

1. Prior to the lesson, create a problem-solving graphic organizer on chart paper with the problem written in the center and the questions in each section. A sample is shown in Figure 6.13.

2. Tell students about a situation that required you to solve a problem. It is important for students to understand that problem solving goes beyond solving mathematical problems. For example:

   On the way home from school yesterday I ran into a problem. I was driving along, and all of a sudden I felt a jolt and my car became hard to steer. I heard a thump, thump, thump. I pulled over to the side of the road. Oh, no! A flat tire! This was definitely a problem. I had to decide how I would solve it. I ran through the options in my head. I could try to fix the flat myself, I could call a tow truck company or a friend, or I could just stand by the side of the road looking helpless. I made my decision—I would call a tow truck company. Within a half hour, I was on my way home! Problem solved.

3. Explain that when we solve everyday problems, we go through a process—we decide what the problem is, evaluate the information, decide on a strategy, solve the problem, and decide if the solution makes sense. Make connections between your story and the steps in the problem-solving process. For example:

   When the car started acting up, I knew I had a problem to solve. After I pulled over and checked the tires, I realized I had a flat tire. I began thinking of strategies to solve the problem, and I decided on one. The tow truck company came and fixed my tire and I made it home—my solution was reasonable!

4. Introduce the problem-solving graphic organizer. As you solve the sample problem, think aloud and record each step of the process on the graphic organizer.

Chapter 6

Figure 6.13 Sample Problem-Solving Graphic Organizer

What does the problem ask me to find?

I need to find the number of pizza slices that can be purchased with $28.

What Information does the problem give me?

The cost of 3 slices of pizza is $12.

Problem

At Pizza Pi food truck, pepperoni slices are 3 for $12. How many slices can you buy with $28?

What strategy or operation will I use to solve this problem?

I can solve the problem by making a table.

How do I solve the problem?

Slices	Cost
1	$4
3	$12
7	$28

What Is my solution? Does It make sense?

I can buy 7 slices of pepperoni pizza with $28. My answer makes sense because $4 is close to $5 and 7 slices at $5 each would be $35. $28 is a little less than $35.

Review and Reflect

1. Reflect on your current classroom routines and procedures for students. How will you adapt them for Math Workshop?

2. What methods do you use to teach students behavioral expectations at the beginning of the school year? Which of your practices aligns with the suggestions for the First 15 Days Plan presented in this chapter? In what ways, if any, might you change your methods?

3. What do you think is most important in preparing students to participate in Math Workshop? Why?

Your Turn!

Now, it's your turn to design Math Workshop for your classroom.

Chapter 1: Structuring Math Workshop introduces various workshop models. Use what you learned to answer these questions:

1. Which Math Workshop rotation model will I use in my classroom and why?

    _____

    _____

    _____

    _____

    _____

2. What will my management board look like for Math Workshop? Sketch your management board with workstation labels.

Chapter 2: Organizing Math Workshop provides a variety of classroom arrangements and tips for keeping materials organized. Consider these questions:

1. How will I arrange my classroom to effectively accommodate Math Workstations? Sketch your classroom, and label the Math Workstation areas.

2. What containers, labels, and materials will I use for Math Workstations, and where will they be stored?

_____

_____

_____

_____

_____

_____

_____

Chapter 3: Managing Math Workshop presents strategies to help establish effective routines and procedures for Math Workshop. Think about what you learned as you respond to these questions:

1. What routines and procedures are important for my students to know in Math Workshop? List five routines and procedures.

    _____

    _____

    _____

    _____

    _____

    _____

    _____

    _____

2. What strategies will I use to motivate my students to be responsible independent learners?

    _____

    _____

    _____

    _____

    _____

    _____

    _____

    _____

Chapter 4: Planning Math Workstations describes effective ways to group students for independent work during Math Workshop and how to create engaging workstation tasks. Refer back to the chapter to answer these questions:

1. What data will I use to identify student needs in order to group students appropriately? Consider both formal and informal assessment data.

    _____

    _____

    _____

    _____

    _____

    _____

    _____

2. What tasks will I include in Math Workstations? List five possible workstation tasks.

    _____

    _____

    _____

    _____

    _____

    _____

    _____

    _____

3. How will I incorporate the use of digital devices into Math Workshop?

_____

_____

_____

_____

_____

_____

_____

_____

Chapter 5: Math Workstation Tasks offers sample tasks that may be easily adapted for use in different grade levels. Explain how you will address the following questions:

1. How will I differentiate workstation tasks for my students?

_____

_____

_____

_____

_____

_____

_____

_____

Chapter 7

2. How will I hold students accountable for their independent work?

_____

_____

_____

_____

_____

_____

_____

Chapter 6: Implementing Math Workshop provides strategies for introducing routines and procedures and new Math Workstation tasks to your students. Refer to this chapter to answer these questions:

1. How will I teach my students the routines and procedures of Math Workshop?

_____

_____

_____

_____

_____

_____

_____

2. How will I introduce new Math Workstation tasks to students?

_____

_____

_____

_____

_____

_____

Review and Reflect

1. What are the first steps you will take to implement Math Workshop in your classroom?

2. With the implementation of any new instructional strategy, there are bound to be challenges. Reflecting on the implementation process, what difficulties or pitfalls do you think you may encounter? How might you address them?

3. When trying something new, it always helps to have support. What kinds of support (e.g., colleagues, coaches, administrators, PLCs, online blogs) are available to you?

References Cited

Bay-Williams, Jennifer M., and Gina Kling. 2014. "Enriching Addition and Subtraction Fact Mastery through Games." *Teaching Children Mathematics* 21 (4). http://www.nctm.org/Publications/Teaching-Children-Mathematics/2014/Vol21/Issue4/Enriching-Addition-and-Subtraction-Fact-Mastery-through-Games/.

Black, Paul, and Dylan Wiliam. 1998. " Inside the Black Box: Raising Standards Through Classroom Assessment." *Phi Delta Kappa* 80 (2): 139–148.

Boaler, Jo. 2014. "Research Suggests Timed Tests Cause Math Anxiety." *Teaching Children Mathematics* 20 (8): 469–474.

Boushey, Gail, and Joan Moser. 2006. *The Daily 5: Fostering Literacy Independence in the Elementary Grades.* Portland: Stenhouse.

Claxton, Guy, Arthur L. Costa, and Bena Kallick. 2016. "Hard Thinking About Soft Skills." *Educational Leadership* 73 (6): 60–64.

Dacey, Linda, and Rebecka Salemi. 2007. *Math for All: Differentiating Instruction, Grades K–2.* Sausalito: Math Solutions Publications.

Davies, Anne. 2000. *Making Classroom Assessment Work.* Courtney, Canada: Connections Publishing.

Diller, Debbie. 2011. *Math Work Stations: Independent Learning You Can Count On, K–2.* Portland: Stenhouse Publishers.

———. 2016. *Growing Independent Learners From Literacy Standards to Stations, K–3.* Portland: Stenhouse.

Fountas, Irene, and Gay Sue Pinnell. 2001. *Guiding Readers and Writers Grades 3–6: Teaching Comprehension, Genre, and Content Literacy.* Portsmouth: Heinemann.

Goodwin, Bryan. 2014. "Research Says/Which Strategy Works Best?" *Educational Leadership* 72 (2): 77–78.

Grinder, Michael. 1995. *ENVoY: Your Personal Guide to Classroom Management.* Battleground: Michael Grinder and Associates.

Hattie, John. 2009. *Visible Learning: A Synthesis of over 800 Meta-Analyses Relating to Achievement.* New York: Routledge.

Hoffer, Wendy. 2012. *Minds on Mathematics: Using Math Workshop to Develop Deep Understanding in Grades 4–8.* Portsmouth: Heinemann.

Koenig, Rhoda. 2010. *Learning for Keeps: Teaching the Strategies Essential for Creating Independent Learners.* Alexandria, VA: Association for Supervision and Curriculum Development. http://www.questia.com/read/124620007/learning-for-keeps-teaching-the-strategies-essential.

Kohn, Alfie. 1993. "Choices for Children: Why and How to Let Students Decide." *Phi Delta Kappa* 75 (1): 8–21. http://www.alfiekohn.org/article/choices-children/.

Marzano, Robert J. 2007. *The Art and Science of Teaching: A Comprehensive Framework for Effective Instruction*. Alexandria: Association for Supervision and Curriculum Development.

MathNook. 2016. "Number Golf." http://www.mathnook.com.

McTighe, Jay, and Ken O'Connor. 2005. "Seven Practices for Effective Learning." *Educational Leadership* 63 (3): 10–17.

Morgenstern, Julie. 2004. *Organizing from the Inside Out*. 2nd ed. New York: Henry Holt.

National Education Association. 2012. "Preparing 21st Century Students for a Global Society: An Educator's Guide to the '4 C's.'" http://www.nea.org/assets/docs/A-Guide-to-Four-Cs.pdf.

National Governors Association for Best Practices and Council of Chief State School Officers. 2010. "Common Core State Standards: Mathematics." Washington DC. www.corestandards.org.

Nichols, Maria. 2006. *Comprehension Through Conversation: The Power of Purposeful Talk in the Reading Workshop*. Portsmouth: Heinemann.

Pearson, P. David, and Margaret C. Gallagher. 1983. "The Instruction of Reading Comprehension." *Contemporary Educational Psychology* 8 (1): 317–344.

Pelton, Tim, and Leslee Francis Pelton. 2012. "7 Strategies for iPads and iPods in the (Math) Classroom." *THE (Technological Horizons in Education) Journal*. https://thejournal.com/Articles?2012/07/11/7-Strategies-for-iPads-and-iPods-in-the-Math-Classroom.aspx?Page=3&p=1.

Ritchhart, Ron. 2015. *Creating Cultures of Thinking: The 8 Forces We Must Master to Truly Transform Our Schools*. San Francisco: Jossey-Bass. Kindle Edition.

Russell, Susan Jo. 2000. "Developing Computational Fluency with Whole Numbers in the Elementary Grades." In *The New England Math Journal*, edited by Beverly Ferrucci and Kathleen M. Heid. 32 (2) 40–54. Keene: Association of Teachers of Mathematics in New England.

Sammons, Laney. 2010. *Guided Math: A Framework for Mathematics Instruction*. Huntington Beach: Shell Education.

———. 2013. *Strategies for Implementing Guided Math*. Huntington Beach: Shell Education.

———. 2014. *Guided Math Conferences*. Huntington Beach: Shell Education.

———. 2015. *Implementing Guided Math: Tools for Educational Leaders*. Huntington Beach: Shell Education.

Small, Marian. 2012. *Good Questions: Great Ways to Differentiate Mathematics Instruction*. 2nd ed. New York: Teachers College Press, and Reston, VA: National Council of Teachers of Mathematics.

Texas Education Agency. 2012. *Texas Essential Knowledge and Skills*. http://tea.texas.gov/index2.aspx?id=6148.

Van de Walle, John A., and Loue Ann H. Lovin. 2006. *Teaching Student-Centered Mathematics*. Boston: Pearson.

Vygotsky, Lev. 1978. *Mind in Society: The Development of Higher Psychological Processes*. Cambridge: Harvard University Press.

PLC Excerpt from Implementing Guided Math

Learning Plan for Month 5

Learning Focus: Supporting Guided Math with Math Workshop

1. Share PLC members' journal reflections from Month 4.

2. Complete the reading assignment and discuss the reflection questions.

3. Select which of the suggested activities for the month the team will undertake and complete them.

4. Record reflections in their personal journals.

Reading Assignment

- *Guided Math: A Framework for Mathematics Instruction,* Chapter 6, pp. 183–205 and/or

- *Strategies for Implementing Guided Math,* Strategies for Math Workshop, pp. 221–276

Reading Discussion Questions

✎ What is your prior knowledge of Math Workshop? What experiences, if any, have you had with it?

✎ For what reasons would you choose to establish Math Workshop in your classroom? What are the benefits to teachers? Students?

✎ What do you think are the greatest challenges in implementing the workshop model?

✎ Why is Math Workshop an essential component of the Guided Math framework?

✎ What routines and procedures for students work best? How should they be taught?

✎ In what ways can students be held accountable when they work independently in Math Workshop?

✎ What types of learning tasks do you think are best for the math workstations? Why?

◆ 223

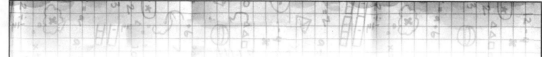

Suggested Learning Tasks

Carousel Brainstorm Protocol

To find solutions for problems encountered when implementing Math Workshop, conduct a brainstorming session using the "Carousel Brainstorm Protocol" (See Chapter 7, page 197).

Peer Observation

Visit a classroom to observe Math Workshop. Record what you observe on the Month 5 Peer Observation Form (See page 226). Share your observations with the team. Add your observation form to your portfolio.

Discussion Questions: Ask the teacher who was observed to describe the workshop model used. What kinds of tasks were in the math workstations? What did students do if they encountered a problem while working independently?

Math Workshop Wiki

As a team, gather various models for Math Workshop and the students' routines and procedures from colleagues and from Internet research. Compile these to create a Math Workshop Wiki that can be used by the entire professional community.

Workstation Show and Tell

Bring workstation tasks you have used in your classrooms or plan to use to share with the group. Also share the routines and procedures you have developed. Explain how you taught them to your students. These ideas may be added to the Math Workshop Wiki. If time permits, work collaboratively to create math workstation tasks for your classrooms.

224 ◆

Month 5 Peer Observation Form
Math Workshop

Teacher Observing _____ Teacher Observed _____

Date of Observation _____

In recording observations, be specific. List what is observed without value judgments.

1. Describe the Math Workshop model you observed.

2. Describe the tasks at each math workstation.

3. Describe the level of engagement of students while working independently. How were students held accountable?

4. What evidence of student learning did you observe?

226 ◆

Additional Resources

The additional resources for each Math Workstation task are included in this appendix. They can also be downloaded and printed from the Digital Resources (see page 19).

120 Chart

1	2	3	4	5	6	7	8	9	10
11	12	13	14	15	16	17	18	19	20
21	22	23	24	25	26	27	28	29	30
31	32	33	34	35	36	37	38	39	40
41	42	43	44	45	46	47	48	49	50
51	52	53	54	55	56	57	58	59	60
61	62	63	64	65	66	67	68	69	70
71	72	73	74	75	76	77	78	79	80
81	82	83	84	85	86	87	88	89	90
91	92	93	94	95	96	97	98	99	100
101	102	103	104	105	106	107	108	109	110
111	112	113	114	115	116	117	118	119	120

Race to the Bottom Spinner

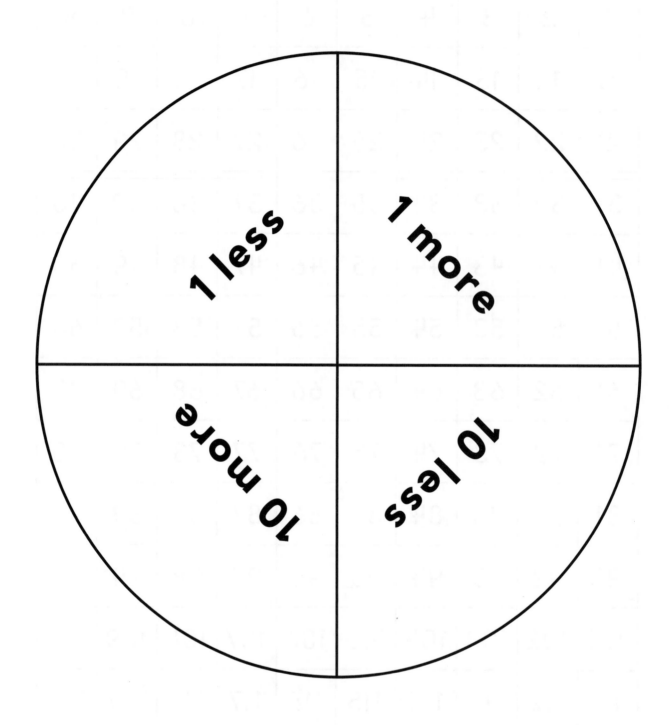

Area and Perimeter War Cards

Area and Perimeter War Cards *(cont.)*

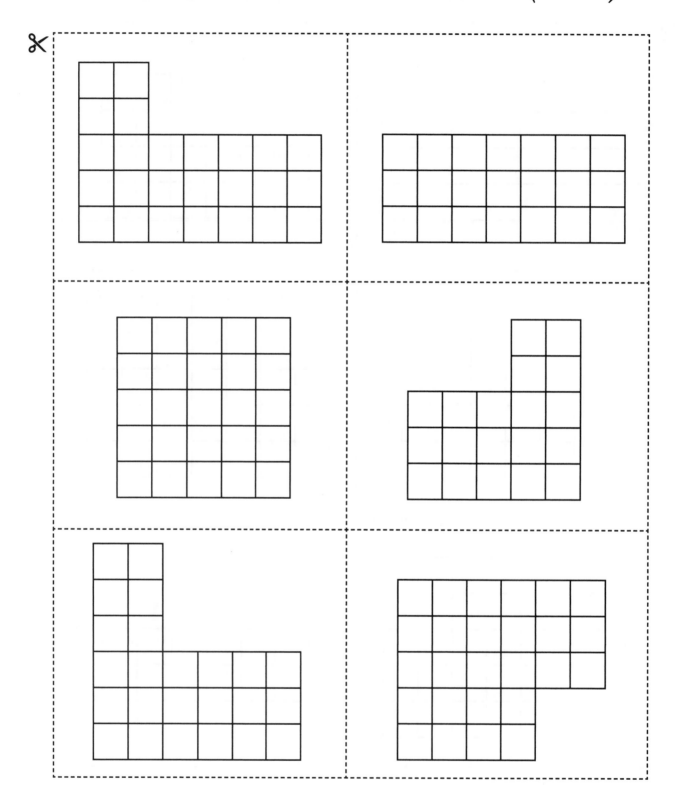

Area and Perimeter War Cards *(cont.)*

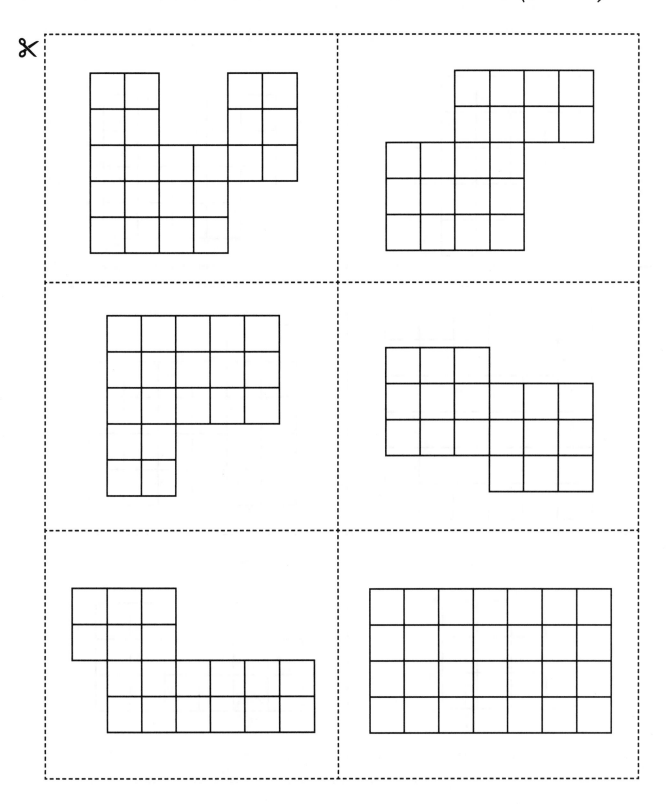

Area and Perimeter War Cards *(cont.)*

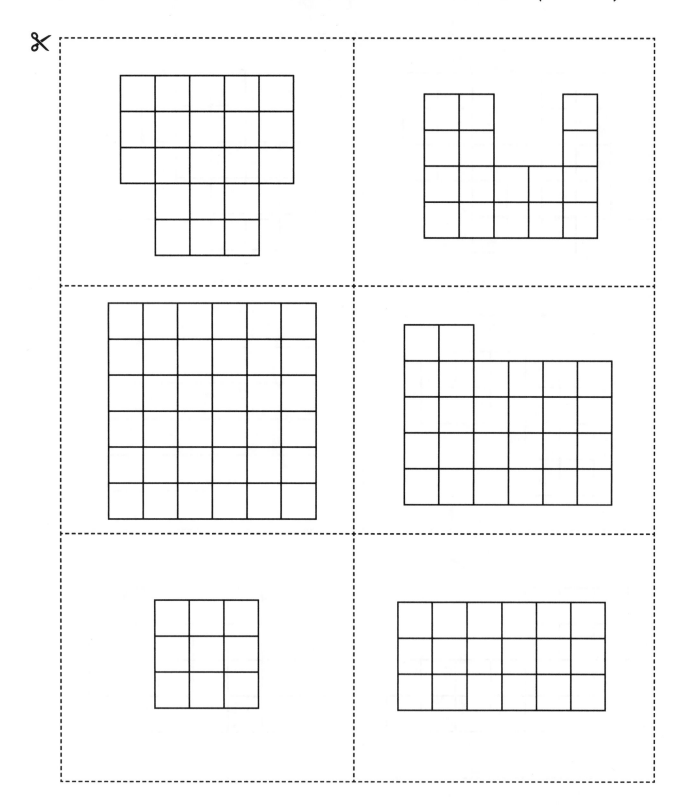

Area/Perimeter Spinner

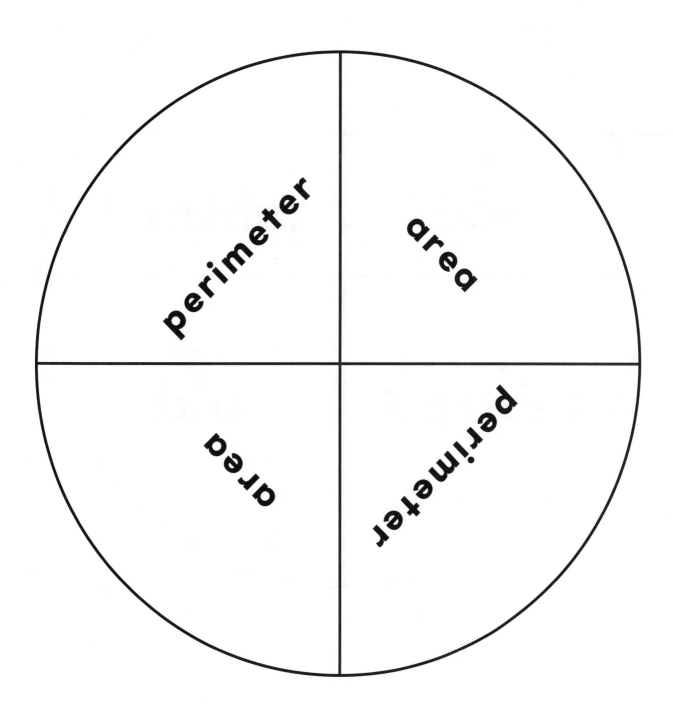

Add/Subtract Spinner

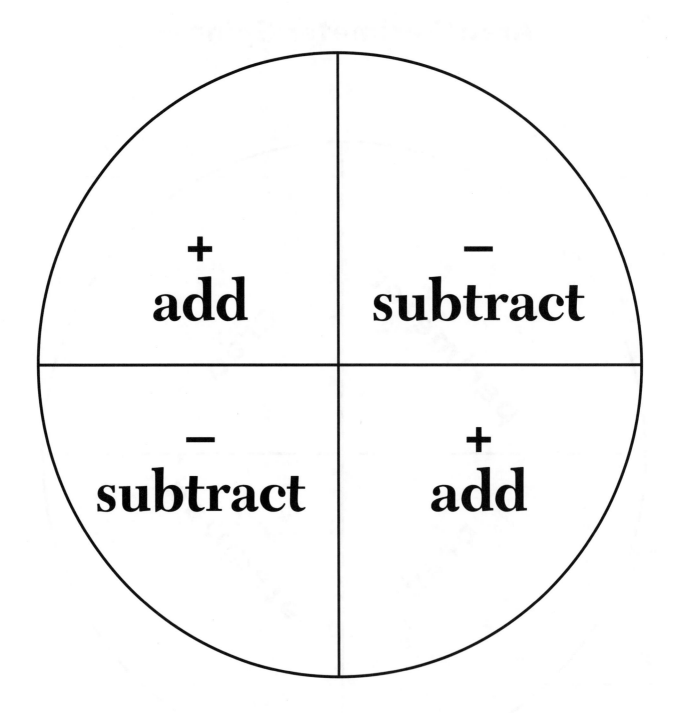

51654—Guided Math Workshop

© Shell Education

Integer Tug-of-War Game Board

Player 1 Home		−1	0	1		Player 2 Home
−16		−2		2		16
−15		−3		3		15
−14		−4		4		14
−13		−5		5		13
−12		−6		6		12
−11		−7		7		11
−10	−9	−8		8	9	10

Name: _____

My Polygon Picture

Write the number of blocks you used.

triangles _____   rhombuses _____   trapezoids _____

hexagons _____   squares _____

Number sentence: _____

Describe the attributes of your polygons.

1. _____

_____

2. _____

_____

3. _____

_____

Piggy Bank Problems Cards

Name: _____

What's the Value?

Directions: Write the coins from your 5 cards in each of the circles. Write the value of the coins using both the cent symbol and a dollar sign and decimal point.

Coins	Cent Symbol	Dollar Sign and Decimal Point
(Q) (Q) (D) (N) (P)	66¢	$0.66
( ) ( ) ( ) ( ) ( )		
( ) ( ) ( ) ( ) ( )		
( ) ( ) ( ) ( ) ( )		

Coins	Cent Symbol	Dollar Sign and Decimal Point

Coin Value Chart

quarter

quarter

quarter

nickel

nickel

nickel

dime

dime

dime

p   p   p

51654—Guided Math Workshop

Rule Cards

△ + 10 = ▢

▱ + 12 = ⬡

◇ + 6 = ◺

⬓ + 8 = ○

▢ + 20 = ⬠

⬗ + 7 = ⬓

○ + 15 = △

◇ + 100 = ◺

Rule Cards (cont.)

⬠ × 2 = ▱

◯ × 4 = ⬡

□ × 5 = ◹

◇ × 7 = ◗

▱ × 10 = ▯

△ × 100 = ⬡

▱ × 3 = ⬠

▱ × 8 = ⬠

Input-Output Cards

Input	Output
1	
3	
9	
12	

Input	Output
2	
4	
8	
10	

Input	Output
12	
15	
18	
21	

Input	Output
4	
12	
24	
30	

Input-Output Cards (cont.)

Input	Output
10	
40	
60	
90	

Input	Output
3	
6	
12	
18	

Input	Output
16	
28	
32	
48	

Input	Output
5	
15	
20	
35	

Name: _____ Date: _____

Follow the Rule Recording Sheet

Rule: _____

Input	Output

Rule: _____

Input	Output

Rule: _____

Input	Output

Rule: _____

Input	Output

Name: _____ Date: _____

Follow the Rule Graphing Sheet

Rule: _____

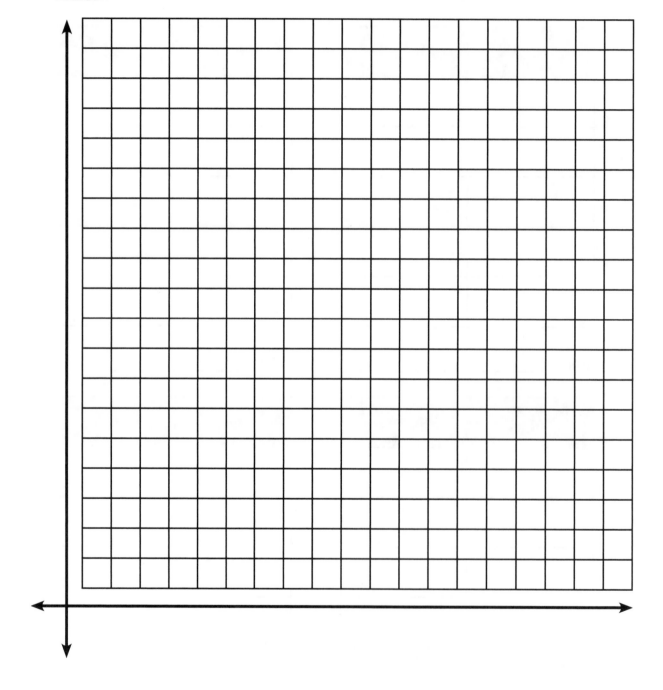

Y-Intercept Cards

$b = -1$	$b = -2$	$b = -3$
$b = -4$	$b = -5$	$b = -6$
$b = 0$	$b = 0$	$b = 0$
$b = 1$	$b = 2$	$b = 3$
$b = 4$	$b = 5$	$b = 6$

Ordered Pair Cards

(−2, 3)	(4, 2)	(3, 5)
(1, 6)	(−3, −4)	(−6, 2)
(3, 1)	(−4, 1)	(−5, −2)
(2, 3)	(6, −3)	(−1, 5)
(−3, 3)	(1, 4)	(4, −5)

51654—Guided Math Workshop

Name: _____ Date: _____

Slope and Intercept Recording Sheet

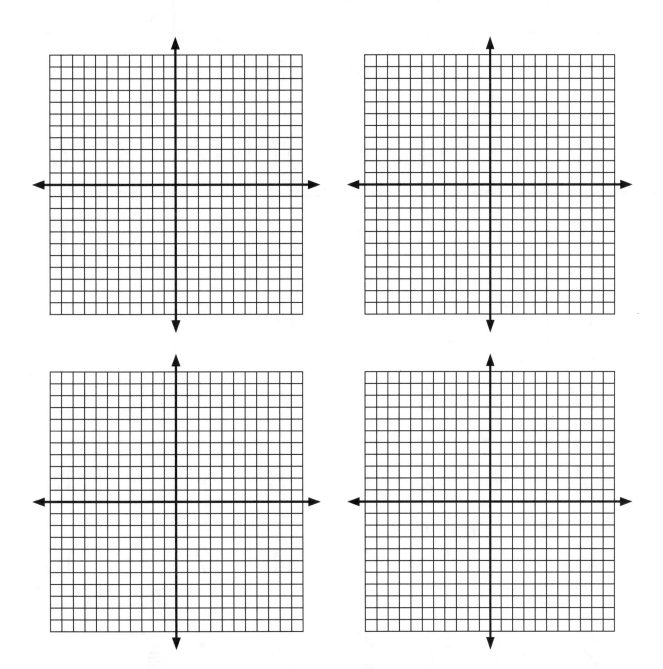

Addition Move One Game Board

11	18	7	13	8	5	10	16
9	5	12	16	18	14	9	17
8	10	14	6	11	12	13	6
14	11	15	10	15	8	16	11
6	13	9	14	17	12	5	17
17	10	16	5	7	15	16	12
7	14	12	15	18	6	9	18
13	7	18	8	11	17	15	10

2 3 4 5 6 7 8 9

Addition/Subtraction Chart

+/−	1	2	3	4	5	6	7	8	9	10
1	2	3	4	5	6	7	8	9	10	11
2	3	4	5	6	7	8	9	10	11	12
3	4	5	6	7	8	9	10	11	12	13
4	5	6	7	8	9	10	11	12	13	14
5	6	7	8	9	10	11	12	13	14	15
6	7	8	9	10	11	12	13	14	15	16
7	8	9	10	11	12	13	14	15	16	17
8	9	10	11	12	13	14	15	16	17	18
9	10	11	12	13	14	15	16	17	18	19
10	11	12	13	14	15	16	17	18	19	20

Number Cards

2	3	4
5	6	7
8	9	10
11	12	

Multiples Tic-Tac-Toe Game Board

Multiples of...

①	②	③
④	⑤	⑥
⑦	⑧	⑨

Alternate Number Cards

20	30	40
50	60	70
80	90	100
110	120	

Scientific Notation Task Cards

Write the number 2,300,000,000 in scientific notation.	Write the number 37,000,000 in scientific notation.
Write the number 68,500,000 in scientific notation.	Write the number 48,000,000,000 in scientific notation.
Write the number 500,000 in scientific notation.	Write the number 705,000,000 in scientific notation.
Write the number 90,000,000 in scientific notation.	Write the number 350,000,000 in scientific notation.

Scientific Notation Task Cards (*cont.*)

Write the number
0.000000345
in scientific notation.

Write the number
0.000024
in scientific notation.

Write the number
0.0000701
in scientific notation.

Write the number
0.0006
in scientific notation.

Write the number
0.00000067
in scientific notation.

Write the number
0.0000005
in scientific notation.

Write the number
0.000000314
in scientific notation.

Write the number
0.0000098
in scientific notation.

Scientific Notation Task Cards (*cont.*)

Express
3.8×10^8
in standard form.

Express
2.06×10^3
in standard form.

Express
9×10^6
in standard form.

Express
6.5×10^5
in standard form.

Express
8.55×10^4
in standard form.

Express
1.4×10^7
in standard form.

Express
1.25×10^5
in standard form.

Express
7.3×10^6
in standard form.

Scientific Notation Task Cards *(cont.)*

Express 5.8×10^{-5} in standard form.	Express 6.22×10^{-4} in standard form.
Express 2.03×10^{-6} in standard form.	Express 7×10^{-3} in standard form.
Express 9.1×10^{-7} in standard form.	Express 1.75×10^{-6} in standard form.
Express 8×10^{-9} in standard form.	Express 4.6×10^{-7} in standard form.

51654—Guided Math Workshop

Scientific Notation Task Cards (*cont.*)

Write the number in scientific notation.	Write the number in scientific notation.
Write the number in scientific notation.	Write the number in scientific notation.
Write the number in scientific notation.	Write the number in scientific notation.
Write the number in scientific notation.	Write the number in scientific notation.

Scientific Notation Task Cards (cont.)

Express in standard form.	Express in standard form.
Express in standard form.	Express in standard form.
Express in standard form.	Express in standard form.
Express in standard form.	Express in standard form.

51654—Guided Math Workshop

Name: _____ Date: _____

Scientific Notation Recording Sheet

Directions: Record the scientific notation and standard form for each card you draw.

Scientific Notation	Standard Form

Name: _____ Date: _____

Scientific Notation Operations Recording Sheet

Directions: Choose 6 cards. Use all 6 cards to complete the tasks below.

Choose 2 of your cards and find the sum.

Choose 2 different cards and find the difference.

Use your last 2 cards and find the product.

51654—Guided Math Workshop

© Shell Education

Operation Cards

+	+	+
+	+	×
×	×	×
×	−	−
−	−	−

My Math Vocabulary Book

Name: _____

Word: _____

What It Means	What It Looks Like

Word: _____

What It Means	What It Looks Like

Word: _____

What It Means	
What It Looks Like	

Word: _____

What It Means	
What It Looks Like	

My Math Vocabulary Book

Name: _____

Word: _____

What It Means	What It Looks Like	Reminds Me Of...

Word: _____

What It Means	What It Looks Like	Reminds Me Of...

Word: _____

What It Means	What It Looks Like	Reminds Me Of...

Word: _____

What It Means	What It Looks Like	Reminds Me Of...

Mathematical Models

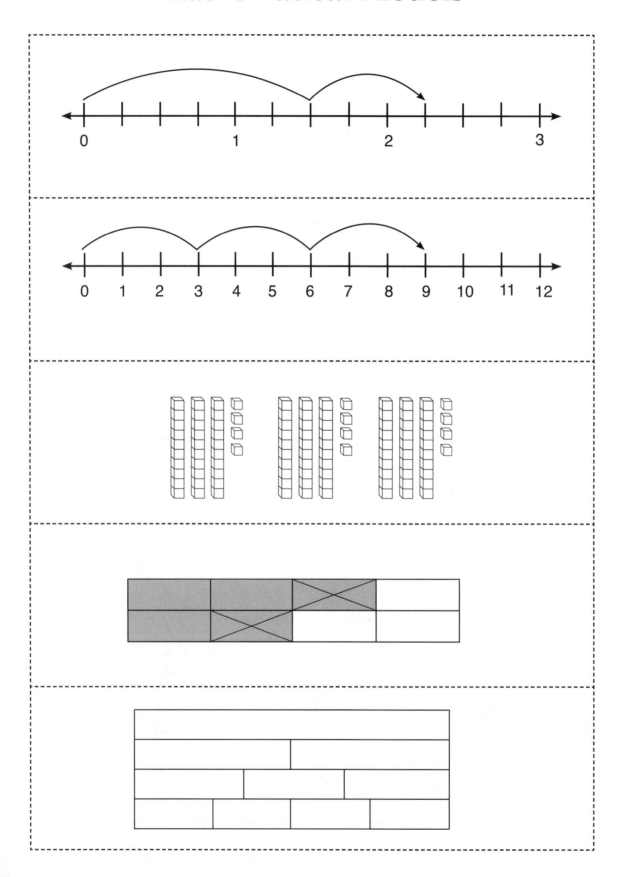

Mathematical Models *(cont.)*

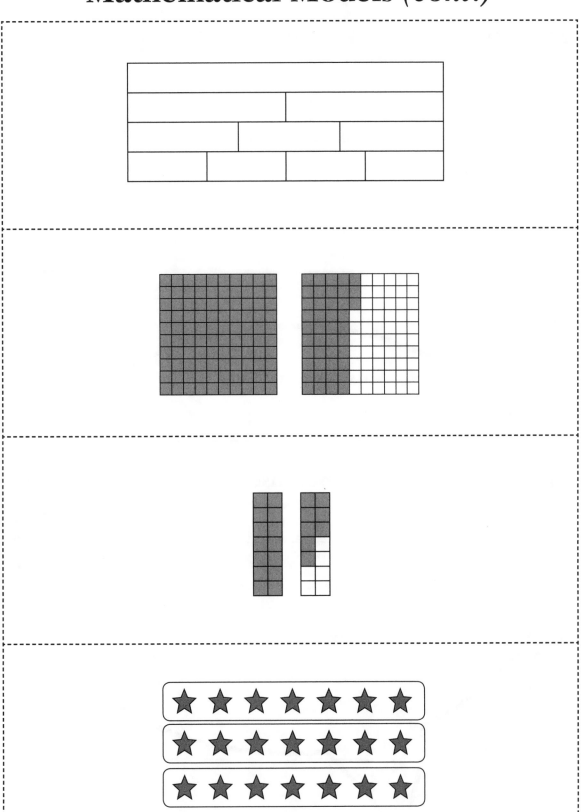

Name: _____ Date: _____

This Reminds Me Of... Recording Sheet

[glue picture here]

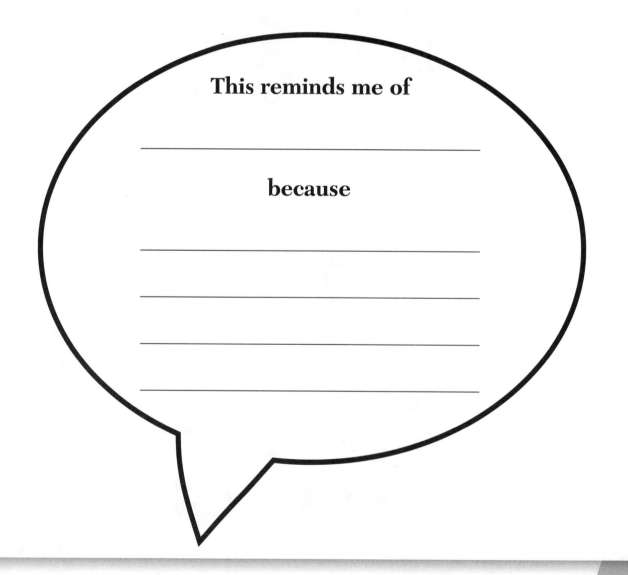

This reminds me of

_____

because

_____

_____

_____

_____

51654—*Guided Math Workshop*   © *Shell Education*

Making Connections Vocabulary Board

	1	2	3	4	5	6
1	area	factor	integer	variable	distributive property	statistics
2	circumference	rational number	right triangle	absolute value	rate	prism
3	ordered pair	equation	spread	quadrant	quadrilateral	polygon
4	probability	percent	inequality	evaluate	protractor	population
5	scale	pyramid	coefficient	ratio	tree diagram	random sample
6	obtuse triangle	supplementary angles	volume	frequency	volume	coordinate plane

Name: _____ Date: _____

Making Connections Graphic Organizer

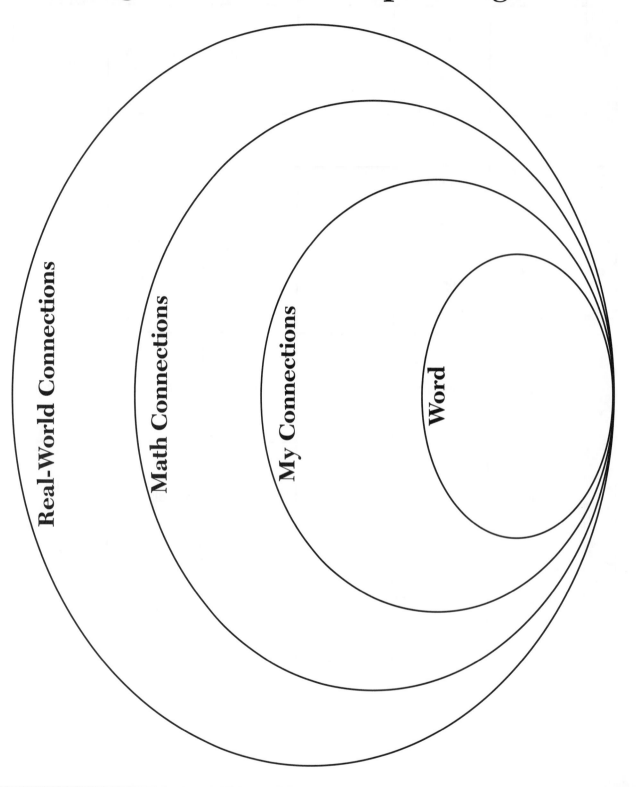

Real-World Connections

Math Connections

My Connections

Word

51654—Guided Math Workshop © *Shell Education*

Name: _____ Date: _____

Compare-and-Contrast Graphic Organizer

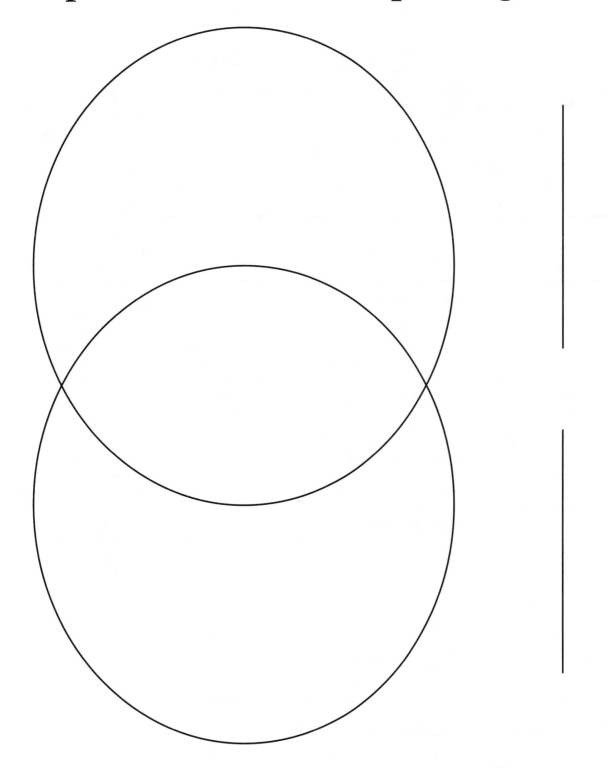

Digital Resources

Page(s)	Resource	Filename
—	Sample GUIDE Workstation Labels	guidelabels.pdf
—	GUIDE Menu Tasks	taskmenu.pdf
—	Recording Sheet (Grades K–2)	recordingK2.pdf
—	Recording Sheet (Grades 3–5)	recording35.pdf
—	Recording Sheet (Grades 6–8)	recording68.pdf
—	Centimeter Graph Paper	centgraph.pdf
—	Think and Evaluate Self-Assessment (Grades K–2)	thinkevalK2.pdf
—	Think and Evaluate Self-Assessment (Grades 3–5)	thinkeval35.pdf
—	Think and Evaluate Self-Assessment (Grades 6–8)	thinkeval68.pdf
—	Expectations Checklist Self-Assessment (Grades K–2)	expectcheckK2.pdf
—	Expectations Checklist Self-Assessment (Grades 3–5)	expectcheck35.pdf
—	Expectations Checklist Self-Assessment (Grades 6–8)	expectcheck68.pdf
73	Race to the Bottom Student Task Card	racetask.pdf
74	Race to the Bottom Talking Points Card	racetalk.pdf
76	Area and Perimeter War Student Task Card	areatask.pdf
77	Area and Perimeter War Talking Points Card	areatalk.pdf
79	Integer Tug-of-War Student Task Card	integertask.pdf
80	Integer Tug-of-War Talking Points Card	integertalk.pdf
82	Polygon Pictures Student Task Card	polygontask.pdf
83	Polygon Pictures Talking Points Card	polygontalk.pdf

Page(s)	Resource	Filename
85	$1,000 House Student Task Card	housetask.pdf
86	$1,000 House Talking Points Card	housetalk.pdf
88	Graphing Growing Patterns Student Task Card	graphtalk.pdf
89	Graphing Growing Patterns Talking Points Card	graphtask.pdf
91	Piggy Bank Problems Student Task Card	piggytask.pdf
92	Piggy Bank Problems Talking Points Card	piggytalk.pdf
94	Follow the Rule Student Task Card	followtask.pdf
95	Follow the Rule Talking Points Card	followtalk.pdf
97	Slope and Intercept Student Task Card	slopetask.pdf
98	Slope and Intercept Talking Points Card	slopetalk.pdf
100	Addition Move One Student Task Card	addtask.pdf
101	Addition Move One Talking Points Card	addtalk.pdf
103	Multiples Tic-Tac-Toe Student Task Card	multipletask.pdf
104	Multiples Tic-Tac-Toe Talking Points Card	multipletalk.pdf
106	Scientific Notation Student Task Card	sciencetask.pdf
107	Scientific Notation Talking Points Card	sciencetalk.pdf
109	Math Vocabulary Book Student Task Card	vocabtask.pdf
110	Math Vocabulary Book Talking Points Card	vocabtalk.pdf
112	This Reminds Me Of… Student Task Card	remindtask.pdf
113	This Reminds Me Of… Talking Points Card	remindtalk.pdf
115	Making Connections Student Task Card	connecttask.pdf
116	Making Connections Talking Points Card	connecttalk.pdf
179	120 Chart	120chart.pdf
180	Race to the Bottom Spinner	spinner.pdf
181–184	Area and Perimeter War Cards	areacards.pdf
185	Area/Perimeter Spinner	areaspinner.pdf

Page(s)	Resource	Filename
186	Add/Subtract Spinner	addspinner.pdf
187	Integer Tug-of-War Game Board	integergame.pdf
188	My Polygon Picture	polygonpic.pdf
189	Piggy Bank Problems Cards	piggycard.pdf
190–191	What's the Value?	whatvalue.pdf
192	Coin Value Chart	coinvalue.pdf
193–194	Rule Cards	rulecard.pdf
195–196	Input-Output Cards	inoutcard.pdf
197	Follow the Rule Recording Sheet	followrecord.pdf
198	Follow the Rule Graphing Sheet	followgraph.pdf
199	Y-Intercept Cards	ycard.pdf
200	Ordered Pair Cards	orderedcard.pdf
201	Slope and Intercept Recording Sheet	sloperecord.pdf
202	Addition Move One Game Board	addgame.pdf
203	Addition/Subtraction Chart	addsubtract.pdf
204	Number Cards	numbercards.pdf
205	Multiples Tic-Tac-Toe Game Board	multiplesboard.pdf
206	Alternate Number Cards	altcards.pdf
207–212	Scientific Notation Task Cards	sciencetask.pdf
213	Scientific Notation Recording Sheet	sciencerecord.pdf
214	Scientific Notation Operations Recording Sheet	scienceop.pdf
215	Operation Cards	opcard.pdf
216–218	My Math Vocabulary Book	mathvocab.pdf

Page(s)	Resource	Filename
219–221	Alternate My Math Vocabulary Book	altvocab.pdf
222–223	Mathematical Models	mathmodels.pdf
224	This Reminds Me Of… Recording Sheet	remindsme.pdf
225	Making Connections Vocabulary Board	connectboard.pdf
226	Making Connections Graphic Organizer	connectorg.pdf
227	Compare-and-Contrast Graphic Organizer	compareorg.pdf

Notes